SIMONE WEIL

SUNY series, Simone Weil Studies
Eric O. Springsted, Editor

SIMONE WEIL

THINKING POETICALLY

Joan Dargan

State University of New York Press

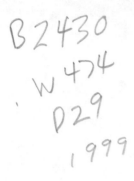

Published by
State University of New York Press, Albany

For information, address State University of New York Press,
State University Plaza, Albany, NY, 12246

Production by Dale Cotton
Marketing by Anne M. Valentine

Library of Congress Cataloging-in-Publication Data
Dargan, Joan.
    Simone Weil : thinking poetically/ Joan Dargan.
        p. cm. — (SUNY series, Simone Weil studies)
    Includes bibliographical references and index.
    ISBN 0-7914-4223-3 (hc : alk. paper). — ISBN 0-7914-4224-1 (pbk. :
alk. paper)
    1. Weil, Simone, 1909–1943.   I. Title.   II. Series.
B2430.W474D29   1999
    194—dc21   98-34052
                                                          CIP

10 9 8 7 6 5 4 3 2 1

For Lynn and Nils Ekfelt

CONTENTS

ACKNOWLEDGMENTS

Grateful acknowledgment is made to Harvard University Press and to Gerald Duckworth and Company for permission to quote excerpts from *Art in the Light of Conscience*, translated by Angela Livingstone. Copyright © 1992 by Angela Livingstone. Reprinted by permission of Harvard University Press.

Parts of this book were published in earlier form as *"Trésor éparpillé*: The Treasure of Scattered Texts in Works by René Char and Simone Weil" in *The Beauty that Saves: Essays on Aesthetics and Language in Simone Weil*, edited by John M. Dunaway and Eric O. Springsted (Macon: Mercer University Press, 1996), and as "Weil and Tsvetaeva on Poetics," *Cahiers Simone Weil* (September 1997).

Opportunities for professional travel and sabbatical leave, all supported by St. Lawrence University, made this work much richer in research and in reflection than it otherwise could have been. These brought me into contact with the community of Weil scholars, American and French—a wonderful, unanticipated benefit of my initial solitary reading. I am grateful to these colleagues for the sharing of insight and for many instances of hospitality and graciousness; I will always cherish the warm welcome I received upon first undertaking research in France, and thereafter unfailingly extended to me, by André and Annette Devaux. I wish especially to thank those who directly helped me as I brought this work to completion: Eric O. Springsted, whose interest in this study was unwavering from the start, and who always stood ready to administer sage advice and doses of optimism as the work slowly materialized; Florence de Lussy, who gave me access to the Simone Weil collection at the Bibliothèque Nationale de France, plied me with books and articles, and cheerfully spurred me on; and Christine Ann Evans, who kindly agreed to read the manuscript in a late version and whose astute suggestions led to great improvement in its organization.

Abbreviations

AD	*Attente de Dieu*
C	*Cahiers* (Plon)
CO	*La Condition ouvrière*
CS	*La Connaissance surnaturelle*
E	*L'Enracinement*
EL	*Ecrits de Londres*
ML	"Morale et littérature"
OC	*Œuvres complètes*
P	*Poèmes, suivis de Venise sauvée*
VSW	Simone Pétrement, *La Vie de Simone Weil*

A Note on Translation

All translations from the French of Simone Weil and other writers are mine, unless indicated otherwise in the list of works cited. Page numbers from the French editions have been retained so that interested readers can readily find the passages in their original form.

INTRODUCTION

Praise of my own [intelligence] has as its very *purpose* to avoid the question: "Is she right or isn't she?" (*EL* 256)

To speak of style and perspective in the work of Simone Weil almost seems to willfully misapprehend her, to escape the intellectual challenge and ignore the moral gravity of the words of so compelling and uncompromising a writer. Even to think of Weil as a writer requires the immediate qualification that she was also much more than a writer, her moral, political, and spiritual journeying venturing upon a terrain far broader than the printed page—a page that is only now coming into its own, with the publication of her *Œuvres complètes* by Gallimard. Those who would know Weil must encounter her there, and, once having done so, few can remain indifferent—can afford to remain indifferent—to the force and clarity of expression given her often unsettling ideas, to the spirit of inquiry and authority that support them. As her friend and colleague Gilbert Kahn has noted: "Given that her project is not strictly philosophical, and despite the interest of her religious ideas and political analysis, Simone Weil would not have the reputation she does today if it were not for that stylistic brilliance evident in her essays and letters and even in her notes" (379). The startling lucidity of her prose and the unswerving conviction with which she speaks are so disarming that one might even think at first that there is no discernible style or point of view in this writing, so diffused and impersonal is the author's presence. And yet one knows such a thing to be impossible.

What other thinker of her time so ardently proclaims the absoluteness of truth, justice, and beauty, and so freely exposes her hunger, sustained by "the guarantee that if one asks one's Father for bread, he does not give stones" (*AD* 87)? It is not only the almost unearthly voice that seems, in the aftershock of the Second World War, incongruous, detached from the overwhelming contingencies of the here and now; it is the subjectivity as well, moving back and forth between human misery, all too near, and the otherworldly. Implacable logic is yoked to yearning; vast erudition fuels the fire of indignation burning in the depths of a scandalized soul. Implicit refusal of identifying, hence limiting, allegiances underlies utterances that would be categorical and universal—passages of astounding beauty and others that appall. At times, nothing less than the complete disorientation of the reader seems to be among the writer's goals. The reaction of Flannery O'Connor upon receiving a translation of Weil's notebooks is one measure of the strangeness of Weil's writing: "I intend to find that *Time* with her picture (some weeks ago) and cut out the picture and stick it in the front. That face gives a kind of reality to the notes" (189). It is no ordinary discursive writing that challenges the reader to associate with it the fact of a human presence; it is a form of provocation—daring one to respond—instead. Weil's use of language is not only, as one would expect, highly sophisticated; it is audacious, stunning, willing to risk offense in the service of expressing, or testing, her convictions. What Hannah Arendt writes of Walter Benjamin applies equally to Weil: "[W]e are dealing here with something which may not be unique but is certainly extremely rare: the gift of *thinking poetically*" (Benjamin 50).

Weil's contempt for those who would fall back on remarks about her brilliance rather than examine her ideas reminds those reading her, littérateurs in our safety, that sometimes the forces engaged in writing eclipse the dimensions of the mere inscribed paper, which may or may not outlast us. To a truth seeker of Weil's convictions, the longing for literary immortality is necessarily as immature as that for any kind of immortality, a subject about which she wished to harbor no illusion: "[I]f death is annihilation, [there must be] two kinds of annihilation, annihilation into nothingness and annihilation into God" (C 3:89). The personal element does not survive; in the "I," there is no eternity. In light of this belief, her philosophy of decreation is simply an unblinking realism. Even in the short run, what must have life at the time of Nazi rule appeared to offer a Simone Weil? A student of politics, Weil had long realized that a hostile world may be all too ready to dispense with the fact of one's being, if doing so were to suit its convenience. In Weil's notebooks, and in her later works in general, one is confronted by the evidence of both a matter-of-fact anticipation of erasure and an awesome explosion of creativity—an appalling contradiction of terms on some level necessarily compatible; a phenomenon reflected in an unbearable tension of tone, an extremism in posture, a chilling dejection. Coming upon the work as an artifact, one may indeed feel the need for a photograph—some concrete evidence—to locate the source of fragments from which the human element seems to have been banished: in these various responses to text and context lie two different kinds of realism, postwar reader's and the writer's.

In his advice to a young poet, Max Jacob wrote: "Make yourself permeable, for how will you achieve lyrical conflagration if you have neither felt nor thought anything" (20). From her year of factory work on, Weil seemed impelled by a similar injunction, and her later work—in its voluminousness, in its thirst for justice, in the relentless incision of its prose—tells us that nothing is more urgent or more difficult to achieve than a sense of our precarious existence in this world. Hers is, as O'Connor says, "the religious consciousness without a religion" (189), thinking and feeling its way alone in the midst of tragic circumstance. Her perspective is novel, in many ways a tribute to the courage of her permeability; it is also unique and often disturbing and historically defined. Looking at her language, how can we see beyond its evident, disarming brilliance to discern the poetic thinking—sign of an individual presence—there? What are the characteristic movements of that thought? What assumptions, aesthetic and otherwise, seem implicit in her style? How is the poetic dimension of her writing implicated in its era? Fortunately, the written page, too, is permeable. We must learn to be sensitive to the forces that underlie its surfaces, to the silences and silencings the phrasing of its thought implies:

> History is based upon documents. A historian will, by profession, refrain from hypotheses that have no foundation. To all appearances this is entirely reasonable; in reality, it is far from it. For, there being holes in documents, the balance of thought requires that unfounded hypotheses be present to the mind, on condition that it be for this reason and that for each point there be several such hypotheses.
>
> It is all the more necessary when reading documents to read between the lines, to transport oneself fully, with complete self-forgetfulness, into the events evoked there, to stop and examine at length the small, revealing things and discern their full significance.
>
> But respect for the document and the professional attitude of historians do not dispose the mind toward this kind of exercise. The so-called historical mind does not pass through the paper to find flesh and blood; it consists of a subordination of thought to the document. (*E* 283–84)

The reader is never powerless; the work is in our hands. How then, according to Weil, are we to proceed? For Weil, historical works, properly read, take us into a space outside the text, between the lines—even, in a sense, beyond ourselves. Starting with an incontrovertible object, a physical piece of evidence, she reveals its porous texture by means of an exercise of imagination and intelligence anchored in the particular detail. History is only refracted in document, and the discerning reader must summon an intangible network of hypotheses and intuitions to counter the factitious authority conferred upon the text. This presence of mind, as Weil sees it, quite literally constitutes intellectual freedom. She is handing the reader a key with which to unlock the work's hidden, and not always innocent, secrets; she is prescribing a kind of attentiveness that will lead closer to the heart—that "flesh and blood"—of human experience all writing imperfectly registers. Her own work invites no lesser consideration; and so with this passage taken as a caution, or rather a challenge, directed to the reader, let us follow her lead.

Weil begins her argument by two seemingly objective, impartial observations, the first of these, "History is based upon documents," expressed in the passive voice and with use of the definite article (in the original French) to indicate general categories. History, documents—these are entities not otherwise in need of specification, one of which provides the foundation for the other. If a hierarchical relationship were to be inferred, one would note the dependency of history upon its surviving products, and specifically on written texts. The practice of history reposes upon the written word and affirms its primacy, its authority. In the following sentence, Weil introduces a human agent, "a historian," but "he" [sic] is not, as one might have expected, introduced as the missing intermediary between "history" and "documents" whose absence had been suggested by the use of the passive voice. If anything, the historian's rigor makes action impossible; by definition, he must, "by profession," scrupulously avoid any deviation from the text, any unfounded conjecture: "hypotheses that have no foundation." His work proceeds by negation, not of what is within the document, but of that which it does not contain. Weil has already exposed stylistically the procedure she will go on to denounce—namely, the subordination of the intelligence of the historian to the piece of paper, the negation of the power of the intellect and imagination, fueled with sympathy, to travel back through time.

Close inspection of the text, Weil observes, will necessarily lead into uncharted territory. The appearance of reason can be a form of safety, of willed ignorance in the face of risk. The perception of "holes" adds to the negativity or nothingness already associated with the treatment of historical documents; documents conjure up with them a kind of forbidden, unspeakable territory that, by convention, professional historians do not acknowledge. Yet such acknowledgment is necessary for Weil, for the sake of "the balance of thought," for the preservation of intellectual integrity. To counterbalance the negative space of omission or distortion, the mind must inquire at every point into other unstated, still to be proved possibilities. It is the equilibrium of thought that requires this; not thought, but the condition of its balance—a quality illustrating an impersonal principle, one essential to its functioning—that magisterially commands the presence of unproven hypotheses as the initial step in substantiating the missing, as yet unidentified elements whose absence from the documented account has been detected.

Weil has exposed the limitations and permeability of the document, along with the uncritical and ultimately falsifying passivity inherent in the prevailing historical method of her day, one responsible for a notion of French grandeur so much at odds with the reality of military occupation. As she describes it, respect, or perhaps more accurately, worship, of the document only paralyzes the reader, forbidding the mind to embark upon hypothetical courses that carefully considered words might open to it. In denouncing the tyranny of the method, she would free the imagination to get up and walk. The profoundly democratic impulse revealed by this affirmation of intellectual freedom is of a piece with Weil's concern for social justice, and her words are a stirring reminder of the dignity of the intellectual enterprise.

The paragraph that follows, clearly describing a personally familiar operation of the intellect, confirms a characteristic movement of Weil's thought simply in the absence of any reference to a personal pronoun. The self is, in the French, "*soi*," the third-person impersonal form. Yet what is more personal, more creative, more interpretative in nature than the action she describes: "It is all the more necessary when reading documents to read between the lines, to transport oneself fully, with complete self-forgetfulness, into the events evoked there, to stop and examine at length the small, revealing things and discern their full significance." Having discerned a lack in the documented sources, Weil would supply a new presence: the mind of the reader fully engaged, to the point of self-forgetfulness, in the text, with the goal of transcending its limitations. It is an affirmation of the discrimination involved in careful reading, for it is the reader who determines where to travel in the space between the lines, which details are significant, and where their complete meaning lies. For Weil, the discernment of the reader takes precedence over the dictates of the document, and the traditional historian's "objectivity" is seen as defective and subservient. Indeed, if tinged with some bitterness, this is an impassioned argument affirming the value of mind over matter, the strength of the intellect over the weakness of evidence, the wealth of the spirit over the poverty of means. Balanced, creative thought will, according to Weil, pierce through the page to meet "flesh and blood," human reality. Yet the humanity she presents is without distinguishing traits.

Weil goes on to note that "history is nothing other than a compilation of the depositions made by assassins concerning their victims and themselves," and that with such information, "[w]hat is called the judgment of history . . . is incapable of judging except after the manner of 'The Animals Stricken by the Plague'" (*E* 284). The received wisdom of history is corrupt, and the folly of accepting it uncritically has its literary illustration in La Fontaine, where the wily and powerful beasts turn upon the inoffensive donkey in their search for a sacrificial victim. If Weil has demolished the written document as a reliable foundation for history, she nonetheless has recourse to it here, in the form of a favorite literary work, a turn in the argument perfectly in keeping with a conception of reading that would apply directly to the appreciation of poetic works.

Weil's criticism anticipates developments in textual analysis and historical criticism in a postwar era all too aware of the insufficiency and unreliability of the written word. Yet Weil did not limit her inquiry to the subject of language, and her work is not distinguished by characteristic doubt or uncertainty. What is significant in the stylistic analysis of this passage, insofar as it is at all representative of her writing, is the way in which syntax and the choice of vocabulary seem in themselves to illustrate and enact the thought under scrutiny, whether in a positive or negative light, and all the while tending to eliminate personal reference in favor of an impersonal form of expression, the latter no doubt associated with the authoritative, sometimes absolute quality of some of Weil's pronouncements. It is this movement toward the impersonal—in a sense, to borrow her own terminology, the linguistic decreation of the self—that is a significant characteristic of Weil's style.

Perhaps writing itself was for Weil a process of decreation, the poetic imagination employed in the service of an impulse toward the universal. But if the universal is a liberating ideal, democratic in its effect, Weil's description of it insists on its unalloyed essence at the expense of any "flesh and blood" characteristics. It is exclusive, rather than inclusive, insofar as the presence of the speaker is concerned. Unobtrusiveness in writing is often a welcome trait; but in Weil there is a certain oppressiveness in the drive to the impersonal, almost a ruthlessness of exclusion with respect to the prerogatives of the voice.

Although she advocates an open-ended, intuitive form of inquiry, a daring one can see from this distance as prescient and courageous, she is ever the rigorous philosopher, typifying the elite produced by the French educational system. This is not to say that her often daunting lucidity is not admirable, but rather that controlled reasoning can be used oppressively. Philosopher Michèle Le Dœuff notes somewhat disparagingly: "In the training we received, 'rigour' only ever meant a way of pruning everything that is not acceptable to all at the outset. It only suppresses that which risks appearing whimsical or freakish. This companion of the wisest conformism (as though wisdom was conformist!) produces both boredom and illusion" (221). If one prunes away too much, one kills the tree. Weil was not a conformist, but she recognized the danger of an all-too-common susceptibility to the influence of groups, present even within herself (*AD* 23–24; *EL* 20). At different periods of her life, and sometimes within the same work, most remarkably in *L'Enracinement* (*The Need for Roots*), Weil's thought moves in ways ranging from the most innovative and unfettered to the most reactionary; the kind of discipline to which she subjected her thinking and her language might be a consistent element in this sometimes disconcerting combination of creativity and repressiveness.

Thus the movement of her thought toward the universal or impersonal is like a double-edged sword, capable of cutting through chains and of shearing off limbs, always razor-sharp. It is ever prepared to clear away obstacles in its path, be these the imperfections of documents or those of the speaker; it reigns supreme. It has a thematic equivalent in the self-sacrifice of the hero Jaffier in Weil's play *Venise sauvée* (*Venice Preserved*), not to mention her proposal to send nurses to the front lines during the Allied invasion of France (the similarity of these works already noted by Fiori and McLellan). In her writing, Weil seems to consider the self an obstruction, an impediment, literally a mote in God's eye:

> I cannot conceive the possibility that God loves me when I so clearly sense that affection for me even from human beings can only be mistaken. But I can easily imagine that he loves that perspective on creation that can only be had from the point where I exist. But I stand in the way. I must withdraw so that he can see. (*OC* 6:2:489–90)

If you would eliminate perspective, you must eliminate the eye of the beholder—and hence the beholder.

This rigorous logic of exclusion leads in a direct line to the infamous anecdote about the merciless Talleyrand that Weil likes to recall: "When the beggar would say to Talleyrand, "But Your Grace, I must live," Talleyrand would reply, "I don't see the need for it" (E 192). Political oppression is a crude imitation of our metaphysical predicament: the necessity of our existence is not apparent; indeed, the nonnecessity of it seems the much more reasonable prospect, as considered from a position of power. At the same time, because it moves beyond consideration of persons, this logic has no traffic with prestige or privilege; it is the same Weil who, as George Steiner notes, met the French defeat with a thought for the necessary rejoicing in colonial Indochina (172), and who remarked that putting out the eyes of a young Watteau and forcing him to turn a mill would be no less a crime than forcing a youth who did have the vocation for such work to labor in a factory (EL 22). It is the same logic that admits, in September 1940, of the usefulness of casting Jews as scapegoats [Devaux (1997), 45–46] and that eight years earlier led her to assist the syndicalists in Le Puy despite public outrage and the ugly personal attacks directed against her.

Weil's work thus contains within it the impetus toward silence (eclipse by a superior force) and an imperative for protest (refusal of received ideas). When the two come into conflict, as in the following passage from her essay "Expérience de la vie d'usine" ("Experience of Factory Life") (OC 2:2:289–307), the whole underpinnings of the writing process are called into question:

It is difficult to be believed when one describes only impressions. But it is not possible to describe otherwise the misfortune of a human condition. . . . Nothing is more difficult to know than misfortune; it is always a mystery. It is mute, according to a Greek proverb. One must be especially prepared for inward analysis to grasp its real nuances and their causes. . . . Even if one is so prepared, misfortune itself blocks this intellectual activity, and humiliation always has the effect of creating forbidden zones where thought cannot venture and which are hidden by silence or falsehood. . . .

If someone coming from the outside does enter into one of these islands and subjects himself voluntarily to misfortune for a time that is limited but long enough to let himself be steeped in it, and if he later recounts what is experienced, the worth of his testimony will easily be contested. It will be said that he experienced something different from those staying there permanently. This will be correct if he has engaged in introspection only or if he has merely been an observer. But if, having managed to forget that he came from elsewhere, will return elsewhere, and is there only for a visit, he continually compares what he experiences for himself to what he can read in the faces, eyes, gestures, attitudes, and words of others, in events big and small, there arises within him a feeling of certainty unfortunately difficult to communicate. (*OC* 2:2:299–300)

Weil's self-consciousness as a narrator is not merely a matter of anticipating objections to her method, one that would bring to the fore those experiences typically omitted from historical accounts. Yet it is that; it is also as if she is undergoing a kind of disorientation on the level of discourse, one perhaps not bargained for in her original plans. Her experience has come to resemble that permeable, misleading document of the historian; indeed, she may have been thinking of the factory as she was writing that passage in *L'Enracinement* some years later. However factory life may be structured, it conceals forbidden zones, can only be grasped in the details, and requires that deeply inculcated habits of thought be left behind. It is as if Weil has been shocked into adopting a stance that is openly subjective and opaque. The narrator steps into the text and is out of place, in the same way that Weil the intellectual has taken it upon herself to enter the Renault plant. Le Dœuff describes her own introduction to feminism in the 1970s in terms that seem close in this regard to Weil's:

[F]or me as a woman philosopher it was also a positive experience of disorientation. When one thinks one has been trained in 'rigour,' which, in principle, forbids one from advancing something which has not yet been entirely thought through and well-founded, the discovery that whispered, impressionistic stories and openly subjective viewpoints can lead the way to an understanding of the most vital things is a real lesson . . . which teaches the following: it is better to allow yourself to start speaking before being completely sure that you can justify what you say; otherwise, you will never speak at all. (221)

Immersed in an entirely new context, the philosopher learns that the familiar kind of thinking used to establish authority—the support of predetermined reasoning, the creation of a kind of airtight construct—is something inflexible and lifeless, not a key to "the most vital things." To have recourse to the old forms of argument, if one would be truthful, will only immobilize the mind and create an ambiguous, pent-up silence. New evidence must be admitted. New discoveries require new voices—something not in the interests of the powers-that-be, for the old forms are revealed as defensive in nature, intended to keep certain things from being known. Weil says elsewhere, "Only the new is striking" (*EL* 191); only the new dislodges the mind from the usual circuits of thought and forces it to discover new paths. If rigorous argument dissolves and the voicing of impressions is heard, new awareness can emerge.

Weil travels back in memory to retrieve her subject, which is properly silent itself; ancient proverbial wisdom, anonymous and distilled, confirms her initial remembered impressions. Silence is one kind of extreme; so is the mind's helplessness, which is total: "[I]t is not possible to describe otherwise," "Nothing is more difficult to know," "always a mystery," "forbidden zones where thought cannot venture." It is misfortune, and not rigorous logic, that stands at the gate and bars adventurous thought entry. Intellectual activity cannot occur; the factory excludes its liberating and democratic impact. Confronting spiritual devastation, the mind has neither the resources to invent convincing argument, nor any use for one; it is defeated.

It has been argued that Weil's portrait is of limited value because it does not correspond to the experience of the typical factory worker, but that objection cannot be used to deny the reality and validity of what she experienced there. And, having set the stage for her study of the workers' oppression, she casts herself as a mediator, someone who will come and submit to the collective silence, and then go give that experience voice in a place where there is no interdiction. She is like Mallarmé's swan of long ago, frozen in the lake, who "remembers it is he/Who is magnificent but without hope of being free/For not having sung of the place to be living/When the sterile winter's ennui was shining" (1:36). In the mind's tortured, silent immobility, one's true identity is forgotten, and song must be lent, later, to the experience by the poet. Weil is speaking, later, not only for the workers, but for herself.

If Weil's personal intervention in factory life has its dramatic equivalent in the account she wrote of it, the oppressiveness she describes has its equivalent in the language she uses. Most obvious, of course, are her references to the narrator throughout the essay in grammatically neutral or masculine terms ("one," "he," masculine singular adjective forms, etc.). To the extent that the narrator is a linguistic construct and dramatic persona, one would want to extend to Weil as author complete freedom to adapt her work as she wills; her intent is not to focus attention on the narrator per se, but on factory life. But because Weil does insist on the narrator's presence in this essay, contrary to expectation, one wonders what lies beyond the choice of words and the sudden intrusion, what might have dictated the choices.

Weil submitted "Expérience de la vie d'usine" in 1941 to a new Catholic journal, *Economie et Humanisme*, apparently at the suggestion of Father Joseph-Marie Perrin, the Dominican priest who served as her adviser in Marseilles as she explored the possibility of conversion. Out of respect for her parents' wish for discretion as the family was waiting to leave France, Weil used a pseudonym to sign work intended for publication (Fiori 224); her final draft incorporates the more optimistic, prescriptive ending requested by the editors, who in the journal presented "Emile Novis" as "a young intellectual," the noun used in the masculine form (*OC* 2:2:285, 549–55). These alterations have the effect of muting the impact of earlier versions of the essay; the narrator's intervention, originally placed just before what had been the final paragraph, no longer lends the conclusion the force of a ringing condemnation. Weil's use of the anagrammatic pseudonym gives the unsuspecting reader no clue that the factory experience in question was the harsher one specifically reserved for women workers. As Siân Reynolds observes of an even earlier (1936) reworking of material from the factory journal: "Where the diary had made it plain in every sentence, syntactically or by content, that the writer was a woman, doing women's work among other women, these distinctions have almost all vanished from [Weil's published work]" (130).

Anne Roche, editor of the essay for the *Œuvres complètes*, notes other significant changes:

Two long quotations by Marshal Pétain were inserted by the review as epigraphs to the article. These could be overlooked as merely opportunistic and characteristic of the time were it not for the fact that a manuscript version by Simone Weil mentions one of them: "The speech given by Marshal Pétain at Saint-Etienne has impelled me [masculine pronoun in the French] to reread the chapter in *Men of Good Will* by Jules Romains, in which life in a factory is described. . . . " The sentence is crossed out up until "Jules Romains." . . . Crossed out by Simone herself, or by Selma Weil, who did not appreciate the transformations and settings made by *Economie et Humanisme* and reestablished a text faithful to her daughter's manuscripts for the 1951 edition [of *La Condition ouvrière*]? (OC 2:2:285–86)

In the case of this essay, publication meant compromise all the more regrettable for Weil's work's having been founded on such fresh and daring premises; she had begun, with a novelist's eye for detail, to say the small things too quickly dismissed as insignificant, that had been untold. Her affirmation of subjective experience, presented as if general and in conventionally masculine terms, has, as Reynolds rightly insists, the effect of "downgrading . . . the historical specificity of women's work. Reading her work it is easy to miss the gender oppression at the heart of it, while registering oppression in the mode that apparently makes most sense: that of class oppression. But both are there" (131). Whereas Weil hopes to bring oppression out into the open, her recourse to the masculine norm obscures the reality of prejudicial treatment. Linguistic conformity falsifies subjectivity. Political conformity corrupts it even further; by her own hand, no doubt at the editors' suggestion, the author feels compelled to incorporate Pétain's name into the text and even credit him with the inspiration to write. When writing ventures from the private to the public sphere, the pressures to conform are no longer merely internal. It is as if the figure of Pétain comes into the essay, even if only for a moment, at the expense of the women workers, Weil among them—or, rather, it is as if the vacuum created by their unsignaled absence invites such a thing to happen. When Weil speaks of "humiliation [that] always has the effect of creating forbidden zones . . . hidden by silence or false-hood," she looks beyond the factory press to the writing table.

The ethical implications of such editing matter because it is difficult to think of a writer who more eloquently upholds the ideal of intellectual integrity, who takes a more just and fierce pride in her independence from institutions and in her fearless and solitary research: "There is no method for knowledge of the human heart other than the study of history taken together with experience of life in such a way that they shed light on each other" (E 292). To learn that her conspicuous, and not entirely welcome, presence in 1928 at the Ecole Normale Supérieure, a bastion of male privilege, was directly indebted to the protest of a woman denied entrance with full student status only two years earlier (Moi 49) may lead to disappointment in the Weil who could declare, albeit at age nine-teen, "I am not a feminist" (VSW 86), and who could later disguise the greater discrimination suffered by women factory workers. One does not want Justice, in the person of one of its most articulate advocates, to be selectively blind.

How ungrateful it would be, in full view of her achievement, to endeavor merely to say that the sharp, terrible, gleaming instrument that is Weil's prose is necessarily flawed, although in becoming mind-ful of the speaker—affixing the image to the frontispiece—one begins to dispel the aura of impenetrability and even anonymity created by her disembodied voice. Instead, let us consider her writing as one field upon which she waged her struggle for transcendence, oppos-ing her sense of the world's fallenness to that of her philosophical and literary forebears, and drawing up plans to redress those con-temporary moral imbalances she was also prepared to analyze meticulously. Let us look at works of hers implicating a poetic di-mension, admitting into her language music, imagery, and possi-bilities of projection usually excluded from philosophical discourse. By inscribing Weil's work into a literary context and tradition, or at least sketching out the possibility for approaching it in such a way, let us acknowledge her artistry, with its evidence of risks taken and of prodigious technical resources always at hand, and with its grounding in a profound sense of vocation, of responsibility to gifts precariously lodged within her:

> It isn't that I feel within myself a capacity for intellectual creation. But I do feel obligations connected with such creation. I am not to blame. I can't help it. No one other than myself can truly appreciate these obligations. The conditions of intellectual or artistic creation are such intimate and secret things that no one can understand them from the outside. I know that artists excuse their bad behavior in this way. But it is something quite different with me. (*AD* 65–66)

On one level, her rejection of "belles-lettres" as such explains why her so-called failure to explicitly develop a philosophical system in large, polished works is, as she would see it, utterly beside the point; for one thing, writing is of interest only to the extent it reflects the truth she posits beyond it ("[b]ut fortunately for us, there is a reflective property in matter" [*CO* 362]); for another, it is in any event a means and not an end ("Great artists are those for whom art is a secondary thing, a means. The others are inferior (Proust)" [*OC* 6:1:108]). Weil's absolutist language would have as its touchstone of reference none of the things of this world, including intellectual structures. Neither do literary forms interest her except insofar as they correspond to the necessity of writing at hand; hence the multiplicity of fragments, the profusion of genres in her work.

Of course, this orientation differentiates her work from that of poets and writers generally. On another level, then, her relation to her literary tradition—language being unquestionably a thing of this world—is never absent the moral dimension; where one can detect influence, or probable influence, there is also argument, the desire to steer the gaze more clearly toward that "reality located beyond this world, that is to say, beyond space and time" (*EL* 74). The pull toward the universal that gives her prose much of its stark and jarring splendor may occasionally come at the expense of the particular, something already seen in her treatment of factory life, but it is a movement of thought consistent with her philosophy and no doubt her experience.

With Weil, as is manifest in this letter written to Kahn in August 1941, everything is on the line:

> Why should I attach much importance to that part of my intelligence that anyone, absolutely anyone, by means of whips and chains, or walls and locks, or a piece of paper covered with certain characters, can take away from me? If that part is the whole, then I am nothing but a thing of nearly no value at all, so why spare myself? If there is some other thing that proves irreducible, it is that which is infinitely precious. I'm going to see if that is the case.... (*VSW* 568)

This sums up her entire project.

This attempt, more suggestive than exhaustive in nature, to anchor Weil's words in the French literary tradition and in her era is intended to describe a means of access, a reader's entry; the work did not come from nowhere, or even from another planet, despite its authorship by Alain's beloved *"Martienne"* (*VSW* 49). Weil's prose style is necessarily distinctive and grounded in a unique perspective. (That she felt perspective itself to be a burden is another matter entirely.) Refreshingly, mystifyingly, her words are rarely predictable; Weil's cast of mind is of the sort that ponders, lingers, amplifies, races ahead, cuts through forests of impressions with aphoristic sweep; one comes across unexpected elaborations of insight and equally abrupt silences. Such writing is never far from poetry.

Immediately apparent to any reader of French is Weil's immense debt, stylistic and thematic, to Blaise Pascal, her notebooks being direct descendants of his *Pensées*. Striking similarities between Weil's meditations on justice in her essay "La Personne et le sacré" (known, inexplicably, as "Human Personality") and corresponding passages from Pascal's work, along with the striking differences between a prayer of his prompted by illness and the prayer for obliteration found in her New York notebooks, may be understood as evidence both of literary continuity and of an adaptation of the classical ideal in prose. Turning to her predecessor, Weil would refurbish a matchless instrument, a philosophical stylus capable of gleaning abysses—one she saw as adequate, at least until her exile from France, to the intellectual task of confronting the contemporary situation.

Another well-known text, entitled simply "Prologue," an account of a mystical initiation, implicitly has roots in the same symbolic territory giving rise to the prose poem as practiced by

Baudelaire, a figure Weil would not have sought to emulate, but whose work, given her education, she could not have failed to know, and to know well. The poetic element in "Prologue," intended by her as a preface to a projected book of unclassified thoughts, connects her inquiry to a presence abandoned in the world, oppressed by the urban landscape, far from "the gentleness of nature" (C 3:266)—ultimately, one not entirely removed from the modern, transgressive temperament underlying Baudelaire's revolutionary collection of prose poems, *Le Spleen de Paris*.

Weil's *œuvre* also stands firmly alongside the writings of her contemporaries; it was Albert Camus who first edited her works for Gallimard, and Czeslaw Milosz proclaimed his long-standing allegiance to her in his Nobel Lecture in 1980. Weil's notebooks written in Marseilles respond directly to the consequences of her country's defeat, calling to mind the wartime journal of poet and Resistance leader René Char, entitled by him *Feuillets d'Hypnos*, purportedly the leaves of the god of sleep. Her poetry and poetics of this period similarly constitute a defiant, unsentimental response to a terrible era. If her poems must strike one as more earnest in nature than inspired, Weil's insights into the moral and spiritual dimension of writing are comparable in their authority and penetration to those of Russian poet Marina Tsvetaeva, living in exile in Paris at the time she wrote her essay "Art in the Light of Conscience." But despite these signs of commitment to the present moment and its demands, Weil parts company with the works of these poets and writers when, in 1942, she submits her "Proposal for the Formation of Front-Line Nurses" to the Free French—proof of an eagerness to leave the written word, and her distinctive voice, behind.

It is as if bearing the stamp of utmost urgency that Weil's work comes down to us, its character seemingly that of a stumbling block—scripture to some, a scandal to others. Weil, who was not a poet, but who wrote with the same self-forgetfulness that makes poetic creation possible, and who, in so doing, risked all, was somehow not able to acknowledge any solidarity with the women factory workers, whose experience she knew well—or, as is sadly known, with the European Jews being murdered by Hitler. Yet in many of her actions such solidarity was implicit. Cutting through much mystification about Weil's "self-exile," Neal Oxenhandler has shown, clearly and compassionately, how "[s]he was fatally alienated from her body, from her tradition and people, as distant from Judaism as she was, in the end, from Catholicism" (192). Her language was perhaps one place she was at home—although not fully even there, striving to bring the personal element to the vanishing point, courting obliteration. It is when she thinks poetically, allowing her singular music, her startling imagery to pierce through the limpid surface of her prose, that she comes closest to us. In reconnecting her to her literary tradition and to a mode of thought and expression indispensable to all who can hear it, we might see beyond the aura of impersonality to the human presence susceptible to photograph or fingerprint, or the equally individual voiceprint of style; and if the desire for perfection cannot equal perfection itself, the trace of the spiritual journey Weil left behind serves to remind us too of the force of circumstance. No creative gift, including the one so astonishingly manifest in her work, is to be taken for granted. Similarly, the flight of sympathy that passes through paper, like the one that is poetry itself, is never simple, easily accomplished, or sure of success:

> No thing human can be thought about if the past is not taken into consideration, and the past is never verifiable. Not an object of investigation. Reproduced by pure conjecture. Hidden by untruth. How then to escape the danger of committing the worst injustices?
>
> *Read* without passion. For when one reads what is suggested by passion, one is never aware of it; one believes one is reading what is written in front of one's eyes. (*OC* 6:2:273–74)

1

"La Personne et le sacré"

Weil's notebooks, scheduled to comprise four full volumes of the edition of her complete works, are in many ways the nervous center of her *œuvre*, a record of a mind's astonishing range and unassuageable restlessness. Unmediated by conventions of narrative or persona or even some kind of classification, as in a thesaurus, this collection of thoughts exposed in their rawness and massiveness may well daunt the reader accustomed to acknowledgment and signpost; the spectacle of headlong, solitary trailblazing such as this can be unnerving. The doctor who operated on the four-year-old Simone for appendicitis and heard her speaking while under anesthesia thought that a child capable of saying all she was saying could not possibly live long (*VSW* 18); similarly, a reader first coming upon the notebooks might be given to wonder with what human specimen they originated.

Acknowledgment and signpost, in the form of literary precedent, may indeed be found for these works in the trace of the vital influence of the *Pensées* of Pascal. It is he whom Weil invokes in her letter of protest of 1940 to the Vichy Minister of Public Education, where she speaks of "[h]aving practically learned to read from the French writers of the seventeenth century, in Racine, in Pascal" (*VSW* 528). During her years at the Lycée Fénélon (1919–24), she already knew parts of the *Pensées* by heart (*VSW* 40); later, at the Ecole Normale (1928–31), she studied with Léon Brunschvicg, well known for his classic edition of that work. To judge by the many allusions in her notes and essays, Pascal's thoughts were constant companions of her own. Both came to their mature writings on religion having undertaken the discipline of thought in other domains; for Weil, preparation came, more positively, in the form of "meditation on the social mechanism" ("And so I wasn't wrong to have rubbed shoulders with politics for so many years" [*OC* 6:2:434, both citations]); for Pascal, it was the study of mathematics and physics ("When I began the study of man, I saw that these abstract sciences are not appropriate to man, and that advancing in them I strayed more from my condition than did others not knowing them" [1104]). Pascal's definition of eloquence (1094) presupposes versatility in the art of persuasion, something reflected in the variety of genres in his work, a characteristic of Weil's as well. It is to Pascal and the heritage he represents that she clings even as life in France becomes impossible for her; would her work have been imaginable without his example? Pascal and Weil wrest much of their philosophy out of the terror and imminency of those sheer "cliffs of fall" familiar also to Hopkins; in the succinct phrase of André A. Devaux, they are "mystics incapable of forgetting that they are also philosophers" ("Simone Weil et Blaise Pascal" 97).

What is a mystic who is also a philosopher to do with language, having been introduced to a realm where it is dispensable entirely? For Pascal, pragmatic in temperament, apology seems to have been the answer. A Platonist, Weil focuses on the mediating function of language as it points to truths beyond space and time.

Although a full-scale comparison of Weil's notebooks and the *Pensées* is beyond the scope of this study, it is possible to examine a celebrated essay of Weil's very much grounded in observations recorded in the notebooks, "La Personne et le sacré" (*EL* 11–44, translated as "Human Personality"), for signs of its stylistic and philosophical kinship to Pascal's meditations on language and justice in the *Pensées*. The divergences between these figures will come more dramatically to the fore in the juxtaposition following of two smaller works, a prayer composed by Pascal at about the time he was working on the *Pensées*, and an exercise in the genre culled from Weil's New York notebooks.

"La Personne et le sacré," a distillation of her psychology of the individual, according to Thomas Nevin (347), begins by criticizing ordinary vocabulary used to describe persons as individuals and ends by upholding the intrinsic virtue of words referring to absolutes such as truth, beauty, and justice. Weil's assumptions about lexical authority and hierarchy of reference (an upper region of absolute truth, a middle region of social reality, etc.) are so far removed from contemporary focus on the unreliability of reference that one is immediately disoriented, as if spun back to premodernity. Just as suddenly, the reader is plunged into contemporary history with an explanation of the French defeat in terms of a metaphysical struggle between two errors: the powerful German idolatry of the nation-state, and the weaker cult of the individual in France (*EL* 18). Similarly anchoring her absolutist discourse to the ground is one of the essay's most startling and poignant illustrations, based on her observation of courtroom proceedings in Rouen, a city she visited several times in 1940 while her brother was being detained there on a military charge of desertion (*VSW* 510):

> As a tramp, accused in court of having taken a carrot in a field, remains standing before the judge who, all the while comfortably seated, elegantly strings together questions, commentaries, and pleasantries, while the other cannot even manage to stammer out a few words: so truth stands before an intellect occupied with elegantly arranging its opinions. (*EL* 32)

This sense of the helplessness of truth as it is dependent on the workings of privilege and prejudice has its counterpart in Pascal:

> Wouldn't you say that this magistrate, whose venerable old age commands the respect of all the people, is governed by reason pure and sublime, and that he judges things after their nature without tarrying over vain circumstances that only trouble the imagination of the weak? See him enter church for a sermon, bringing his wholly devout zeal, the ardor of charity in him

reinforcing the solidity of reason. Now he is ready to listen with exemplary respect. Let the preacher come forward, let nature have given him a hoarse voice and an odd-looking mien, let his barber have given him a poor shave, suppose he had accidentally gotten his clothes dirty on top of all that, whatever great truths he may announce, I'll bet on our senator's loss of gravitas. (1116–17)

An undercurrent of outrage electrifies the cool, limpid surface of Weil's prose, actually a reworking of a previously stated image: "There is nothing more dreadful, for example, than seeing an unfortunate stammering in court before a magistrate making fine pleasantries in elegant language" (*EL* 14). That Weil's mind circles around the spectacle of social injustice—or, more precisely, burns a circle around it with her scandalized prose—tells us that this is not something to be argued away in reasoned discourse; it is an obstacle, pure and simple, to the truth. Weil's tramp, who must inevitably bring Chaplin and Beckett to mind, is a real tramp, caught in his predicament, accused of wrongdoing in the manifestation of his hunger; is that not the crime, she implies, an offense above all against propriety, for he is hauled up against a mechanism disproportionally weighted against him and his deed. Elegance, ease, fluency, an abundance of verbal entertainments: the judge has in his possession all the marks of privilege that dispose the mind to regard justice itself as another plaything. The inarticulateness of the vagabond, alone, standing, reduced to the desire for a carrot in a field—always the minimum—calls out for the sympathetic ear in the way a historical document demands imaginative reading; but the intellect, professionally engaged, wants only matter for diversion. To be disrupted by need, above all a need upon which one's own wealth is arbitrarily predicated, will not do. The scene is static, the very drama is in the impasse; the tramp remains standing, the judge does not hear. The sketch suffices. Injustice does not care what features we wear.

Pascal's scathing portrait of hypocrisy condemns the social man whose self-satisfaction leaves no room for any other dimension. It is not so much truth's abjection as the official's deficiency that he exposes in evoking a darkly comic scene reminiscent of the Molière of *Le Tartuffe*. Indeed, the scene dissolves into social comedy—the unseemly mirth presumably unleashed at the end—and the false sagacity of the man has been revealed as shallow conformity to the popular image of virtue. One is reminded of Weil's kindred observation that most of the time "people confuse attention with a kind of muscular effort" (AD 90). The magistrate has merely gone through the motions of gravity, as will be proved by his unguarded lapse into levity.

Addressing the reader directly, Pascal's narrator draws us in, has us applaud this worthy figure along with the crowd, follow him as he enters the church and imagine his solemn concentration. We are told of his age and lofty spirit in inflated language rich in cliché ("venerable old age," "reason pure and sublime," "a wholly devout zeal," etc.); his inner qualities are translated into physical posture and expression. These attributes evoke not a specific individual, but a type we may be expected to recognize; we assent to the character's existence, we join in the suspense as he awaits the approach of a suitably dignified preacher. But Pascal confounds our expectations, along with the magistrate's; the preacher offends by his appearance; he has violated the social code crudely and so warrants ridicule, which the magistrate, personifying all that is conventional, all too predictably will supply. We who are alert to the magistrate's inflation might be susceptible to the same response. Our complicity with the narrator, whose worldliness shows through his jaded willingness to bet, also reflects ambiguously on us.

Neither Pascal nor Weil lets the reader off the hook. To the extent that we are social beings—and Pascal meets us on that ground—we are supercilious, knowing, and sorry. We are characters in the drama of social life, however unremarkable our presence. In Weil's fleeting scenario, we may merely be as spectators in the courtroom, but the injustice we may witness there is only replicated in the sordid recesses of our minds. Both writers are confrontational; Pascal, not so much prophet as peer, accompanies us in the exploration of our common folly; Weil leaves us alone with our thoughts, perhaps already condemned by those elegantly arranged opinions.

Equally appalled by officialdom's self-serving deafness to the truth, Pascal and Weil are moved to create striking and related illustrations that also reveal differing rhetorical purposes and hopes of efficacy. A closer look at passages on another common theme, the unarguable existence of evil, will show how deeply ingrained are these differences in voice and temperament, even as the prose of these thinkers gives an overwhelming sense of a shared fundamental outlook and cultivation of a classical style. One of a number of texts in the *Pensées* represents the point of view of the skeptic:

> *Pyrrhonism.* Each thing here is partly true, partly false. Of essential truth this is not so; it is wholly pure and wholly true. This mixture dishonors and annihilates it. Nothing is purely true, and therefore nothing is true understood in terms of pure truth. One might say that it is true that murder is evil; indeed so, because we have knowledge of evil and falsehood. But what will be said to be good? Chastity? I say not, because the world would come to an end. Marriage? No, abstinence is superior. To refrain from all killing? No, because horrible disorders would ensue, and the wicked would kill all the good. To kill? No, because that destroys nature. We have the truth and the good only in part and mixed with evil and falsehood. (1148–49)

Weil, sure of the "natural alliance between truth and affliction" (*EL* 32), never abandons her lofty perspective:

> Truly evil enters into someone upon whom evil is inflicted—not merely pain or suffering, but the very horror of evil. Just as men have the power to do good to one another, so they also have the power to do evil. One can transmit evil to a human being by flattering him, by providing him with well-being and pleasures; but most often men do evil to others by hurting them. (*EL* 39)

Pascal's speaker is the picture of confidence. He uses the pronoun "we" to assert what he takes to be incontrovertible fact; he signals his presence by the pronoun "I," unhesitating in the outline of his argument; the hypothetical interlocutor, identified as "one," joins in the process, providing welcome stimulation. The various implied parties weave a cloak of highminded and animated discussion that becomes an end in itself, neatly hemmed and lifted above the ground. There is no disagreeable contact either with one's colleagues or with unflattering earth. The barter of commonplaces transparent in such thinking simply reflects the social preference for accommodation, confirmed by the circularity of the argument; no real progress occurs. Pascal knows his enemy.

Like the Pyrrhonist, Weil herself, in the passage from *L'Enracinement* cited earlier, has occasion to resort to obvious fact ("History is based on documents") and invoke a hypothetical presence ("a historian") whose position differs from her own. But she will not delay her argument to engage in imaginary dialogue with him; his method having been proved deficient, it is, one gathers, for the historian to perceive the error of his ways, not for her to bring him along (Weil's didacticism and Pascal's are not identical). Similarly, in "La Personne et le sacré," Weil does not invent dialogue or posit consensus. Yet, like the skeptic, she stands before the problem of evil and crafts a statement based on knowledge of human behavior. One might readily imagine the first four sentences attributed to the Pyrrhonist coming from her pen.

In her depiction of social forces, Weil attempts no synthesis, simulates no suspension of belief. She uses indefinite, impersonal pronouns and references to expose the solitude of the individual. Like Pascal's speaker, she alludes to the disposition to cause harm but speaks only of "men," declining to divide them into "the wicked" and "the good" (a distinction that contradicts the skeptic's own conclusions). She bores through the social shell, for Pascal fertile material for the invention of types, to the undiluted horror that is her subject. "[S]omeone," "a human being," the unidentified victim hurt by "one," an unidentified transgressor—the maimed creature has no ready, automatic persona. The Pyrrhonist steps forward into the arena of shared, rational discourse, confident he will not be devoured there, a knowledge of human nature his weapon. Weil's faceless sufferer has already been dealt the fatal blow, other human beings its instrument. The drama is now wholly interior and forbids speech.

The skeptic, incurably detached, approaches the objects of his curiosity as essentially static, using the verb *"être"* (to be) in the conditional and present tenses. The multiple choices at his verbal command—chastity, marriage, killing, not killing—require no commitment on his part. In Weil's darker vision of human possibilities, such distance is illusory. Action occurs inevitably, if in the form of indirection and transfer. Evil itself penetrates; men have given powers; but in acting upon another person (never with that person, there is always a recipient), they redirect an impersonal element (evil, harm, potentially the good) and redistribute it quantitatively, as if obeying a hidden mathematical principle. Even grammatically, the victim becomes the indirect object of evil, subordination illustrated by the language ("someone *upon whom* evil is inflicted," "transmit evil *to a human being*"). The present tense illustrates the operation of a fixed process, an immutable law observed as from on high. For Weil, this world is "here below," always in opposition to the reality beyond. Pascal is content to have his Pyrrhonist speculate "here."

It is Pascal who will venture into the compromising mind of his skeptic, a figure not far removed in spirit from the glib, unfeeling magistrate of Weil's remembered courtroom. Perhaps his gift for social satire was something she would have rejected for herself on moral grounds, inasmuch as it requires the willingness to entertain the possibilities of illusion and evil through fictional constructs. Her writing has a monotonous quality she freely sought. Her interest is in the spiritual laws akin to mechanical ones; she would analyze the working of forces, rather than represent the thought or behavior illustrating those forces. Her style is thus impersonal; one might say, willed to be impersonal, as Weil does not enter her text as narrator, although most certainly she inhabits it. Excluding the personal element, she arrives directly at what is for her the common denominator, that part of the soul susceptible to the horror of evil. This minimalism born of devastation is of its era. Weil's mute, uprooted victim is an unseen brother or sister of Beckett's tramps, and her excruciating attention to the mind's smallest movements recalls the project of Nathalie Sarraute. In his essay "The Power of the Powerless" (1978), Václav Havel reaches a conclusion in language that can fairly be called Weilian: "There are times when we must sink to the bottom of our misery to understand truth, just as we must descend to the bottom of a well to see the stars in broad daylight" (89). But it is Pascal, after all, who freely avers, "The heart has its reasons reason knows nothing of" (1221); our logic and fictions desert us before that human abyss hidden within. Weil is of the company of those writers and philosophers who have the courage to look over the edge of that lifeline so finely spun out by their pen.

The constant refrain of "La Personne et le sacré" is the question, "Why am I being hurt?," first mentioned as that "childlike cry Christ himself could not hold back" (*EL* 13) and an unmistakable sign of injustice. The emergence of explicitly Christian references—there are others to the *Pater* (*EL* 38), the crucifixion (*EL* 41), and Christ's instructions to his disciples (*EL* 43)—shows the strength of Weil's claim to the heritage of Pascal; as if recourse to these references were unremarkable in the midst of impersonal, absolutist language derived from Plato, the implied equation of Christianity with the universal goes without comment. In a sense, the assumptions reflected here are those represented by the whole enterprise of her *Intuitions préchrétiennes*, where she casts Hellenic inspiration as the main, self-evident precursor of Christianity, with no recognition of Judaism as a source. The postwar reader is necessarily troubled by the exclusive religious reference in an exposition collapsing the historical dimension into an insignificant atmospheric layer seen from the lofty view of the supernatural. Must all suffering be inscribed in a Christian context? Can one pry away the essence from the temporal sheath? Weil clearly believes so. Positioning her *cri du cœur* "at the intersection of Christianity and everything that is not [Christianity]" (*AD* 54), Weil brings into apposition vocabulary and references from multiple sources, confirming Oxenhandler's perception of her "as someone who, in the struggle to become whole, drove herself mercilessly to reconcile various fragmented narratives" (8).

This kind of tension necessarily absent from the *Pensées*, Pascal asks a similarly phrased question with far greater rhetorical freedom:

> "Why are you killing me?" "Well, then, don't you live on the other side of the water? My friend, if you lived on this side instead, I would be a murderer, and killing you this way would be unjust; but since you live on the other side, I am a brave man and this is just." (1151)

This is a dialogue reminiscent of La Fontaine; in "Le Loup et l'agneau" ("The Wolf and the Lamb"), for example, having just been accused by the wolf of slandering him a year ago, the innocent lamb protests:

> "How could I have done it if I hadn't been born?
> I'm still nursing even now," the lamb answered.
> "If it's not you, then it's your brother."

"I have none." "Then it's some one of you,
For I am never given a moment's peace
By you, your dogs, your shepherds.
I've been told all about it; I'll have my vengeance." (44–45)

The personification of viewpoints made possible by dialogue is a
useful tool for the social critic. The hapless traveler and the murderer, the lamb and the wolf each confront and address their an-
tagonist. Social behavior is unmasked and distilled, as is, in these
illustrations, the transparent rationalization accompanying the act
of murder; the language of passion mimics logic and stakes desire's
unreasoning claim. In Pascal, question is met by question; geographic
accident is given status equivalent to justification for murder. The
victim is silenced, his cry drowned out by the predator's volubility,
the facile piling up of words betraying the argument's lack of
substance. One need not travel as far as Plato; justice resides on
the other side of the water, as on the other side of the sky. Pascal
also says: "When it is a matter of judging whether one should go
to war and kill so many men, condemn so many Spaniards to
death, it is a lone man who decides, one with an interest; it ought
to be a disinterested third party" (1151). An impartial third party
is best able to decide the fate of the Spaniards or of the man from
the other side of the water. When the subject is injustice, a narrator not himself a party to the scene he describes is best able to
reveal it for what it is.

Weil provides a very different setting for her figure's query:

Justice consists in ensuring that no harm be done to others.
Harm is done to a human being when he cries within, "Why
am I being hurt?" He will often be deceived once he tries to
understand what evil it is he is experiencing, who is inflicting
it upon him, why it is being inflicted upon him. But the cry is
infallible. (*EL* 38)

If justice proceeds by negation, preventing action, injustice is
also known by negation, by the absence of relationship. The attempt to understand—to rationalize, to intellectualize—is likely to
be thwarted. The inner voice speaks, but the sufferer does not confront the evildoer directly. Disruption prevails. The question in

French, *"Pourquoi me fait-on du mal?,"* specifies a self *("me"),* an anonymous agent *("on"),* and a certain quantity of harm or evil *("du mal").* Weil distinguishes between this outcry and the apparently related question of why this harm is being inflicted; attempting to answer the latter question ensnares the mind in the realm of actions and their consequences, the social world dissected so effectively by Pascal and La Fontaine and from which justice has departed. Searching actively for explanation, one only deceives oneself. Only the original question has the ring of truth, of being an immediate response to brute reality. The question posed by Pascal's victim elicits more words and exposes their hollowness; Weil's leaves its speaker in solitude, susceptible to error after the ordeal, but for now exposed, all defenses torn away. She even uses in this instance the conventional masculine persona, itself a form of alienation and exclusion. Forced to contemplate the impersonal connection of the self to the reality of evil—precisely the content of Weil's question—the sufferer finds within "infallible" evidence of an inner life. There is no need for an interlocutor.

Writing in London in 1942 and 1943, Weil must have drawn strength from Pascal's example and fully appreciated the timeliness of his reflections. If she avoids the extended exercise in personification, this may be by way of a correction, refusing to let her thoughts dwell unnecessarily in that middle region where rights, individuality, and the institutions of democracy come into play (*EL* 30). Yet even in a summary description, her impulse is dramatic; there is presupposed a watchful, overseeing presence—an enlightened Creon?—whose role is to prevent miscarriages of justice. When vigilance fails, the unheard cry of wounded innocence—the sign of Antigone?—resounds inwardly. (Weil herself supplies the allusion elsewhere in the essay [*EL* 25–26].) Why is it that Weil's illustrations tend to presume the classical unities of time, character, and situation without also fleshing them out for the reader? Pascal revisits the story of Cain and Abel, writes in the active voice and invents lively discussion. Weil reduces the human element to immobility, adopts the passive voice and uses impersonal forms of reference; later in the essay, she even eliminates human reference altogether ("When the injury has penetrated deeply. . . . " [*EL* 39]). Injustice as a mechanism reveals how negligible our rights and persons truly are. Unlike Pascal, Weil does not even stop to unveil its arbitrary workings; taking its existence for granted, she grammatically reproduces its actions. Personality is erased; the reality of pain supervenes.

Even in their treatment of the theme of spiritual hunger, Pascal's freer use of different registers and Weil's linguistic austerity make themselves apparent. In Pascal, we read:

> One never grows weary of eating and sleeping every day, because hunger is reborn, as is sleep; but for that, one would grow weary. In the same way, without the hunger for spiritual things, one grows weary of them. Hunger for justice: eighth beatitude. (1155)

Once again, Pascal uses "one" to allude to representative behavior; he appeals to a general understanding of human psychology. He leads from common experience (eating and sleeping) to common sense (the return of hunger and fatigue preventing boredom) and on to the moral dimension, by way of analogy. Our passion for justice is the logical outcome of our hunger for it; since this hunger is a spiritual good, deprivation is necessary. The cyclical nature of our appetites, physical and spiritual, wards off disinterest and ensures our attentiveness to the maintenance of good health. We are so constituted that even the things of the spirit ("spiritual things") could not of themselves attract our attention without the fluctuating register of their presence or absence. By this image a kind of quantitative measure is implied, as if the demands of justice regularly moved up and down a sliding scale, one located within the self. Registered as a lack, justice makes us take up its cause again. That this mechanism does indeed exist, and is validated, is confirmed by textual authority.

This passage, at first glance, might seem to have come as easily from Weil's notebooks as from Pascal's; the aphoristic language, the reference to essential needs, the abstraction from experience ("hunger," "justice"), the passage from physical reality to the spiritual— all of these characteristics of thought and expression are common to them both. At the same time, Pascal's call for a certain reasonableness in treating questions of the absolute would be anathema to Weil. The expression "spiritual things" would no doubt strike her as vague and even offensive; for her, absolutes would not enter so readily, linguistically or otherwise, into commerce with our notion of things or objects. Without very explicit qualifications, the expression would be an oxymoron or a base compromise. Weil's preoccupation with the theme of hunger shows her inclination to conceive of questions in the same terms, but Pascal's illustration would probably strike her as repellent. How, she would ask, could one possibly compare justice to an appetite that is routinely satisfied? Her withering remarks on Pascal's wager (*E* 314–15) leave no doubt of her scorn for what she perceives as his willingness to traffic between material and spiritual realities, without attending first to the unyielding demands of intellectual integrity. If the hunger for justice, even if sanctioned in the gospels, essentially staves off a kind of boredom, how can it be worthy of praise, anymore than a yawn before bedtime or an empty stomach before breakfast? Is justice to be reduced to the dimensions of our routine cravings?

If Weil's perspective can be construed as unfair to Pascal, it is in part because she does not admit of considerations of social well-being (different in kind from questions of social order and justice) in the pursuit of truth, and in part because her unstated point of departure differs radically from his. The passing suggestion that the lack of justice, like the lack of food or sleep, is somehow good for us, even in the context of describing a psychological mechanism, would be unacceptable to a thinker just as eager to identify and describe such mechanisms, but who would not categorize them in terms of human behavior. Pascal's approach is more anthropological and prescriptive; his observation of how and why people act as they do is worldly and acute; his argument in favor of the appetites, his advocacy of the wager, would have us capitalize on our limited strength and perception to better our condition. It is not that Pascal loses sight of the nothingness of human beings so eloquently decried in the first pages of the *Pensées*; it is rather that he sees human dependency on God a natural corollary of our situation. Our predicament has its meaning or solution in that dependency; once we have grasped it, and its implication of the soul's ultimate reality, we may orient ourselves and our actions in the right direction. Hopefulness is inscribed in such a viewpoint. For Weil, human misery confirms our dependency on God's absence, and that bitter reality does not logically imply any hope for progress or solution. Her mysticism, which is situated not in humanity per se, but strictly in the individual, and probably passing, soul, does not contradict that fundamental observation. Our appetites do not betray us, they serve us, in Pascal's scheme. In Weil's, they are frankly irrelevant as manifestations of our human nature.

Returning to "La Personne et le sacré," one finds a passage reminiscent of Pascal:

> Beauty is the supreme mystery in this world. It is a brilliance that attracts attention but gives it no motive to stay. Beauty is always promising and never gives anything; it creates a hunger but has in it no food for the part of the soul that tries here below to be satisfied; it has food only for the part of the soul that contemplates. It creates desire, and it makes it clearly felt that there is nothing in it [beauty] to be desired, because one insists above all that nothing about it change. If one does not seek out measures by which to escape from the delicious torment inflicted by it, desire is little by little transformed into love, and a seed of the faculty of disinterested and pure attention is created. (*EL* 37)

Weil speaks of a hunger that draws itself to our attention; she uses the impersonal pronoun "one" in generalizing our response to it; her language, like Pascal's, is striking in its lapidary concision and marvelous use of symmetry. Where he surprises with his reference to "spiritual things," Weil catches us off guard with hers to a "delicious torment." The spiritual hunger for beauty is among those allowed for in Pascal's rumination, one that comes over us again and again.

But in Pascal's world, it is perfectly consistent for such a hunger to exist alongside our natural instincts; its dailiness, its ordinariness, has roots in human nature; it is part of a pattern that identifies us and redeems us. Such a hunger is an instance of right orientation in the midst of human grandeur and misery. It creates an expectation, his analogy implies, that can be satisfied; spiritual things sustain the soul, just as food and sleep sustain the body. Without entirely contradicting Pascal—again, their closeness is often remarkable—Weil proceeds differently. Where Pascal acknowledges the presence of spiritual and material things in the world, Weil lays the emphasis on our being *ici-bas*, here below, where things of the spirit are not so readily accessible. It goes without saying that Weil is more peremptory in her rhetoric; she does not cower before superlatives ("the supreme mystery"). Pascal cites what is commonly acknowledged about the body before going on to assert the existence of a spiritual appetite. His language allows room for contrast (body-spirit) and hypothesis ("but for that, one would get tired of it"); it is an exploration of possibility. The mind tests and affirms the limits of its empire, as does, in the context of his own evil will, the murderer of the man from the other side of the river. One dares to assert within the limits of what is possible; through our language, our actions, we go forth into the world; we participate in the larger thought and action around us. Weil leaves an entirely different impression.

Indeed, in the passage chosen, and again and again in her notebooks, one has the sense of approaching the absolute zero of motion—the effect of undertaking a microscopic examination of the forces at work in the movement of the mind. She speaks from on high, presents an unchanging, static precept ("beauty *is*"). Energy is demanded but given no fuel; the well-balanced engine of the appetites proposed by Pascal is nowhere to be found. Beauty, as Weil conceives of it, would not participate in this process ("there is in it no food for the part of the soul that tries here below to be satisfied"). This hunger does not correspond to ordinary human changeableness; it provokes the desire that nothing be changed ("one insists above all that nothing about it change"), and it is itself not necessarily quickly replaced and forgotten. It may even be transformed, not merely exhausted and reinserted into the cycle of appetites and desires. Weil goes on to find illustrations of the beautiful in great works of literature, linking words to this process.

In Weil, desire is provoked from without ("a brilliance that attracts attention"); it is not unleashed by a sense of lack found within. Thus the source responsible for setting the working of desire in motion is, in Weil, situated outside the self, as if to establish the insignificance of the individual and his or her characteristics from the outset. No pattern of human behavior is of interest. Weil's use of paradox confirms that the phenomenon proceeds quite independently of our expectations ("no motive," "never gives anything"). Beauty does not serve our purposes. The separation of this world ("here below") from supernatural realities is mirrored in the division of the soul between its active, devouring lower part and the part capable of contemplation. Weil steers the self along an increasingly featureless path; the operation is independent of ourselves as well, referred to in terms of "attention," "the part of the soul that contemplates," "one." If there is no resistance—the only action envisioned—beauty simply works on the soul in a manner akin to photosynthesis. A transformation occurs; the attributes of the particular plant are beside the point. Questions of personal or collective identity do not interest Weil in this context.

This impersonal rendering of an invisible phenomenon predicated upon the immobility of the subject, on the renunciation of action, startles by its absoluteness; on what authority, on what observation does this analysis rest? The speaker has dissolved into the prose, though her presence is clearly signaled by the words "delicious torment," a characterization of a state implying full familiarity with it. The "if" clause, introducing not a hypothesis, but rather an observation, likewise arises from personal observation; it calls to mind Weil's allusion to a mediating figure—the role she envisioned for herself—in the factory ("If someone, coming from the outside, penetrates . . . "). The passage strikes with the full force of the author's inner certainty, and the absence of persona in conjunction with the description of such intimate subjective experience disorients the reader. One has the sense of intruding upon the sanctuary of the speaker's mind—but of course it is the speaker herself who has brought us inside.

In the notebooks and later essays where Weil alludes directly to her mystical experience, the combination of breathtaking certainty of tone and erasure of personality in her expression poses multiple challenges to the reader living in what Sarraute calls "the age of suspicion." Even with his classical restraint, Pascal does not remove his moral and spiritual imperatives from the context of space and time and human nature. His predicament is ours; he wishes to persuade us; his words engender self-recognition (we are like the hypocritical killer, we know the pattern of our appetites, etc.); although the cultural context is now far removed, we understand that his writing is offered in the spirit of language being a shared commodity. It is the natural medium of exchange, and just as he quarrels with Montaigne and Descartes in the course of his reflections, so he expects the reader to come to his or her own conclusions. He does not claim to have the last word; the conversation will go on. These assumptions are not necessarily those we would automatically adopt in reading a contemporary text, but we acknowledge the implicit faith in language and in the meeting of minds that has traditionally led to the making and reading of books.

Weil would object to dissection of her style—its elegance, too, like that effect of beauty that draws attention to itself—on the grounds that it is the substance that should be debated: "Praise of my own [intelligence] has as its very *purpose* to avoid the question: 'Is she right or isn't she?'" (*EL* 256). But in many ways her style is exclusive, shutting the reader out. The disappearance of an "I" might well have the effect of concentrating the mind on the discussion at hand, allowing the invisible speaker shaping its boundaries to escape notice. Where, in such shifting terrain, is the reader to stand? Clearly, we are not elevated to the status of interlocutors; made to peer into a mind's private workings, we are to submit to teaching based on that mind's authority. Weil's knowledge is all of a piece, "a massive block" (*EL* 250), and we are to take it or leave it. This attitude of laissez-faire might seem to resemble Pascal's, but he reassuringly shows us that he is seeking truth along with us. Weil has found it and remains at the summit.

Weil's declamatory style—her speech ex cathedra—thus seems to have at least two sources: her inner conviction and the nature of the experience addressed. The impetus for her writing is not discourse; it is silence. Her words are not first and foremost launched by and into the stream of writings begun by philosophers before her and continuing through time (historically speaking, of course they are). One has instead the impression of her traveling a vast inner distance back to the level of language, resurfacing, and then meticulously describing her experiences. Rather than a continuing affirmation of speech, such writing stands in relation to silence; it emerges out of wordlessness. The sense of violation or intrusion we sometimes feel in reading Weil is created by the very fact of recourse to language—with all its inherent limitations, the problem of motivation (Why must such things be formulated at all? Is Weil's motive merely pedagogic?), the reference to experience not every reader could possibly be expected to verify. It is also due, perhaps, to a sense that we might not be her intended readers. As early as her essay *Reflections on the Causes of Liberty and Social Oppression* (1934), Weil foresaw her civilization's demise and articulated the need to begin salvaging what was worthy of preservation. Perhaps Weil intended her texts for future archeologists of the Western spirit, seeing no reason to posit imminent dialogue in a collapsing Europe. Do we come upon these later works of hers too early—again, provoking the sense of exclusion—even if we do not mistake their apocalyptic tone?

Weil's writing is, in passages such as the one under consideration, akin to poetic works in their nature and musicality; sound emerges from silence, of an inner necessity, and returns to it. In an essay like "La Personne et le sacré," and certainly many times in *L'Enracinement*, Weil moves between different levels of experience and correspondingly different kinds of speech. At one moment she may prescribe judicial reform, at another comment acidly on class hypocrisy, and at another draw on mystical insight. The bases of her logic and argumentation are constantly shifting, in ways sometimes unannounced and sometimes obtrusive, delighting or disconcerting the reader. For this reason, one may prefer the freedom and lack of forced connection offered in the reading of Weil's notebooks; her procedure seems at odds with the implied rhetorical consistency and argumentative intent of the philosophical essay, and the formal question can be troublesome. For example, the conclusion of a delightful essay on school studies reinserts all of her previous remarks on the joy and profit inherent in study in an exclusively Christian context, appropriate for what was, in fact, a *pièce de circonstance* written for the use of Father Perrin, but potentially jarring for other audiences. The change of context must inevitably expel some readers; Pascal's prose, in the concerted rhetoric of *Les Lettres provinciales* and in the fragments of the *Pensées*, does not give rise to such conflict. It is part of Weil's originality that thoughts that would be at home in John of the Cross are brought to bear in her consideration of pressing social concerns; it is clear that she believes in the urgency and universality—the truth—of these thoughts and so wishes to privilege them, to place them at the center of her thinking; but it is not so clear that the assertions themselves and the terms used to express them are in fact so obvious and unobjectionable. A reader might well feel compelled to question the overwhelming number of unqualified pronouncements in Weil's prose, all the while admiring her courage and taking instruction from her stunning insights, of which there are many in "La Personne et le sacré."

Indeed, Weil's prose in her later writings—audacious and pro-vocative in her choice of vocabulary, in her fluctuating registers, in her enveloping perspective (in its uninhibited freedom reminiscent of the omniscience of narrators of nineteenth-century fiction)—seems to be located at a crossroads where the exhausted forms of a dying civilization must be discarded at last. It is the Pyrrhonist appearing in Pascal's meditations on justice who anticipates this weariness: "Each thing here is partly true, partly false. Of essential truth this is not so; it is wholly pure and wholly true. This mixture dishonors and annihilates it. Nothing is purely true, and thus nothing is true, understood in terms of pure truth" (1148–49).

Could one come any closer to Weil than in these first lines of Pascal's exposition of the chosen point of view? The Pyrrhonist will not proceed to aspire to the absolute, but the spectacle of the mixed state of good and evil in this world ("here")—in which this world and the mind are imprisoned—arrests his attention just as it does Weil's. However, once he has ascertained this condition, the con-frontation with reality degenerates. He can affirm nothing; the ar-gument does not advance. The meandering, world-weary, inconclusive voice perfectly reflects the theme. Author and persona are distinct; Pascal creates a shadow voice—not his own, and yet his own creation. In this way, that is to say, dramatically, attention is drawn to the persona—or, more specifically, to the caliber of mind that would think this way. This is another example of the ability to adopt different guises and kinds of speech used by Pascal in the service of his quest for truth; the impassioned believer has the imagination to enter into the mind of the skeptic; the philosopher testing the limits of knowledge can wield the language of those who refuse to take up arms.

Pascal in his prose is, like Weil, an adventurer. He will, for the sake of argument, flesh out positions that he considers untenable, momentarily abandoning his own point of view. He will wield the tools of logic and reason to advance into new territory, embracing the unknown in the same way he does different personae. Unflinching in his contemplation of human injustice, he will find use for it; "this infinite chasm" (1185) within us, and which we are constantly tempted to evade through distraction, is nothing other than the trace of "an infinite and immutable object" (1185), some-thing we should seek to possess. His concept of the wager, which

Weil finds utterly lacking in intellectual integrity, celebrates risk and action. Advocating initiative, built upon the language of appropriation, Pascal's call to conversion is the polar opposite of Weil's assertion that it is God who descends to us, if we implore him to. Pascal, who believes in divine miracles, still has confidence in his kind, in the activity of the intellect, in words; Weil, who would entertain no notion of compromise with reality, is fundamentally, as David McLellan calls her, the utopian pessimist.

She presents a completely different picture of the flawed state of the world, in which good and evil, beauty and imperfection coexist:

> Beauty is sensible, although quite vaguely and mixed with many false imitations, inside the cell in which all human thought is at first imprisoned. Truth and justice with their tongue cut out can hope for no other help than its help. It too has no language; it does not speak; it says nothing. But it does have a voice with which to call out. It calls and indicates justice and truth which are voiceless. As a dog barks to bring people to the side of his master lying lifeless in the snow. (*EL* 37–38)

The prison or cave of the mind is precisely where Pascal's Pyrrhonist resides; the impotence of "truth and justice with their tongue cut out" is illustrated by his dispirited negations. But Weil, speaking, like Pascal, of a limited understanding, does not represent the thinker him- or herself; instead, she personifies the ideals thought should aspire to. She endows them with a voice; but truth and justice have been mutilated. Beauty has sound, but not speech; language has been mutilated; there is a forceful series of negations, different in kind from the Pyrrhonist's. Beauty's impingement upon the consciousness, at first vaguely felt and then insistent and effective ("it calls and indicates"), culminates in an image dissociating voice and animation. The process reverses the order of events of that other account of an awakening, Rimbaud's prose poem "Dawn"; the narrator first encounters nature in its stillness ("Nothing was yet moving . . . The water was dead"), only to notice its quickening as he advances ("I walked, awakening the quick and warm breaths"), and soon meets "a flower who told me her name" (140). Nature is an enchanted image of the poet's powers. In Weil, the prison cell of ignorance is abandoned for a desolate landscape in which the state of emergency is plain. That the intelligence is dormant, exposed to the elements, its future doubtful, has a special resonance in light of Weil's allowance that she might honorably be baptized in the event that her intellectual faculties were no longer intact (*AD* 66). The barking dog—absent human speech and reflection—cries out the soul's need, the frozen snow an imminent basin.

Weil's images of deprivation are shocking and violent, deliberately so. In her notebooks, she writes of the writer's need to be as calculating as a coquette in playing with the reader's imagination (*OC* 6:1:320). The tension in this passage resides in the overwhelming implication of the author in the text—Weil would be that voice beauty provides to elicit concern for justice and truth—and the rigorous exclusion of any reference to that implicit presence, even to the obliteration of an image of consciousness. Are we but accidental and, in the event, absent bystanders to an essential, unheard drama that plays itself out without reference to the intelligence? Must the mind, trapped in its restlessness and confusion, be stunned into motionlessness in order at last to perceive? What does the staggering quantity of writing by a brilliant mind mean in the context of this symbol of ultimate despair in discourse? Pascal's leap of faith, undertaken at the urging of reason and hopefulness, is not even conceivable here; truth and justice are sinking in the snow.

More is at stake than merely the disposition toward pessimism. Reading Weil's thoughts on justice in light of Pascal, one is reminded that the horrifying abyss within can have, and most certainly has had, its equivalent without. Like a seismograph, Weil's writing appears responsive to historical pressures, revealing the inadequacy of inherited forms to the moment, the need for new modes of expression. Her language is at the breaking point: breaking into that desolate silence with an always articulate cry, but the words themselves sometimes seem uncomfortably in place. Images of fixity and stillness contrast with the instability of levels of discourse within a given passage. Impersonality of reference—a kind of ruthlessness—coexists with impassioned argument. Absoluteness of conviction and self-annihilation are at one and the same time espoused by the narrative voice. Universality and Christian reference are presented as indistinguishable. In "La Personne et le sacré"—the title itself perhaps indicative of the distance she intended her voice to carry, of the distinction between levels of being she strove in her writing to transcend—mere words are asked to bear the impossible burden of containing absolutes, expunging levels of reference that are inferior. To Weil, this is not an absurd demand; it is a necessary one: "The tree is quite truly rooted in the sky" (*EL* 30).

This is the thought Weil will go on to develop and expand in the aptly entitled *L'Enracinement* (referring not to the need for roots, but to the taking of them). If trees are not really rooted in the ground, in this earth, how much less must we be: "I feel that it is necessary, that it is prescribed for me to be alone, foreign, and exiled from every single human milieu without exception" (*AD* 26). A great anguish is unleashed, personal and metaphysical. It is in part an echo of Pascal's terror before "the infinite immensity of the spaces [of eternity past and future] I do not know and which do not know me" (1113); it resonates with the same despair of human justice flowing from the knowledge that self-interest "is a marvelous instrument for agreeably putting out our eyes" (1119). "La Personne et le sacré" is the cry, "Why am I being hurt?," writ not large, but indelibly and with moving penetration. In another work calling to mind Weil's mystical and philosophical predecessor, the cry becomes more singular still.

2

"The Terrible Prayer"

Weil's notebooks include an "example of prayer" (*CS* 204–6), written in New York in 1942, that has stopped many readers in their tracks, among them her friend and biographer Simone Pétrement. It is clearly marked an example, as if a sort of literary performance; there is even the direction, "Say to God" (204). Although addressed to the Almighty, the discourse is fully controlled by its immediate creator; the parallel structure of its two major parts reflects the evident consciousness of craft involved in its creation. The petitioner is identifiably masculine, grammatically speaking, in keeping with conventional usage and Weil's own sometimes questionable practice. Such artfulness implies detachment. But, the reader may be given to wonder, is prayer ever meant to be an exercise in detachment?

With its chilling and explicit call for self-annihilation, Weil's text seems a complete reversal, denial, or even travesty of the notion of prayer. Nevin cites it in arguing Weil's internalization of the anti-Semitism of Vichy France (287); and, although Weil would have her speaker be anonymous and representative, the insistent repetition

41

characteristic of the text suggests a more than hypothetical identification with him on the writer's part. Is the fierce contempt for the body conveyed by this work a form of betrayal—of the self, of a rejected heritage and people—or is it an exaggeration of a Jansenistic tendency derived from Racine and Pascal? Is the prayer simply an exercise of the freedom to explore a genre, to invent a persona not meant to be interpreted as a literal extension of the author's self?

Before exploring these possibilities, let us look at the first part of "the terrible prayer," as it is called by Pétrement (639):

> Father, in the name of Christ, grant me this.
>
>   That I might be beyond any condition to make any movement of my body, even any hint of movement, obey any of my wishes, like a total paralytic. That I might be unable to receive any sensation, like someone totally blind, deaf, and deprived of the other three senses. That I might be beyond any condition to put two thoughts together, even the very simplest ones, by the slightest thread, like one of those complete idiots who not only do not know how to count or read, but who were never even able to learn to speak. That I might be insensible to any kind of pain and joy, and incapable of any love for any being and for any thing, not even for myself, like aged persons gone completely senile.
>
>   Father, in the name of Christ, truly grant me all this. (*CS* 204)

Framed by nearly identical injunctions addressed to God the Father, "in the name of Christ," the first part of the prayer lists a series of requests that, in any other context, would be so many curses. In them, only the "I" is present; God is as though dismissed, his usefulness consigned to effecting the transformation. No dialogue, no relationship unfolds; in effect, God becomes the speaker's own instrument, called on to create what he—not God—has imagined. If Weil elsewhere condemns the use of prayer in the effort to obtain one's personal ends, here she has contemplated its use in the service of an appalling kind of wish-fulfillment. The speaker writes his own script and asks the divine to be complicit.

In her essay "L'*Iliade* ou le poème de la force" ("The *Iliad* or the Poem of Might"), Weil unforgettably elucidates the way in which might reduces human beings to mere things. In the process of irreversible change she pictures here, God is equated with the blind, brute force of destruction. God too has been blunted. This is not the divine, impersonal force often cited elsewhere who set the material world in motion and then withdrew; this is not Siva, the destroyer, mentioned in the notebooks, who works with indifference to individual desire. The prayer posits a Father who would entertain and grant such a wish; the scenario is perhaps reminiscent of Weil's favorite fairy tale, "Marie of Gold, Marie of Tar," in which the heroine who chooses the least desirable option goes on to receive the greatest reward. Here, however, God makes no decree; all arbitrariness, all tyranny originate in the speaker.

And yet Weil's text is, as she announces it to be, a kind of prayer, the wish for bodily affliction calling to mind, as Eric O. Springsted points out, the desire expressed by Julian of Norwich to be stricken by illness so as to receive her heavenly visions (81). More likely as a direct source for Weil, who had begun reading him by December 1941 (*VSW* 596), is John of the Cross, a frequent reference in her notebooks; she would have known his teaching that "a man must strip himself of all creatures and of his actions and abilities (of his understanding, taste, and feeling) so that when everything unlike and unconformed to God is cast out, his soul may receive the likeness of God, since nothing contrary to the will of God will be left in him, and thus he will be transformed in God" (116). For both these earlier mystics, this voluntary mortification prepares the soul for divine visitation and as such is to be desired. In her written exercise, Weil is elaborating the kinds of debility one might conceivably invoke as part of such preparation, but whereas Julian specifies physical sickness and John of the Cross alludes to a deliberate emptying of the self, Weil dwells more on the condition of mental incapacity, one predicated upon divine intervention. Weil's familiar association of immobility with the truth—pictured as the dog's fallen master in "La Personne et le sacré" (*EL* 38)—reappears in the evocation of total paralysis in the prayer; the petition to be struck dumb and incapable of reasoning recalls also from that essay her likening of wretched sufferers to a person whose tongue has been cut out and who goes to speak, having momentarily forgotten his mutilation (*EL* 36). There is an undercurrent of violence in Weil's prose one does not find in this passage from John of the Cross that might also have served as a model:

An individual, by depriving himself of his appetites for the delights of hearing, lives in darkness and emptiness in this sense faculty.

And depriving himself of the pleasure of seeing things, he lives in darkness and poverty in the faculty of sight.

And denying himself the fragrances pleasing to the sense of smell, he abides in emptiness and darkness in this sense faculty.

Then too by denying the palate the pleasures of delicious foods, he is also in the void and in darkness in the sense of taste.

Finally, by mortifying himself of all the delights and satisfactions of the sense of touch, he likewise dwells in darkness and in a void in this faculty. (76)

As in Weil's prayer, this outline of the kinds of renunciation necessary in the anticipation of mystical experience is built on the use of parallel structures; here, the effect created is one of orderliness and completeness, corresponding to the practice described. The repeated evocation of darkness and emptiness is like a refrain, its conclusiveness born of experience. With each of her petitions, Weil instead introduces similes, creating a picture more vivid and more terrible: "like a total paralytic," "like someone completely blind," "like one of those complete idiots," "like aged persons gone completely senile." John of the Cross speaks directly and authoritatively of a practice that leaves the senses intact; Weil would approximate—hence her recourse to simile—a phenomenon she envisions as a shock, a form of ruin. The Spanish mystic communicates a sense of balance with each sentence: there is acknowledgment of the pleasure and delight associated with a given sense, even as there is the prescription of depriving it of any object. No insult is made to the Almighty's creation. Weil seems to sense the imbalance in her own initial paragraph and goes on to recast her petitions in a positive light, though in imitative prose lacking the power to dazzle or offend:

Let this body move or be still, with perfect fluidity or rigidity, in uninterrupted conformity to your will. Let this hearing, this sight, this taste, this sense of smell, this sense of touch receive the perfectly exact imprint of your creation. Let this intellect, in the fullness of lucidity, connect all ideas in conformity to your truth. Let this sensibility feel in their greatest possible intensity and in all their purity all the shades of pain and joy. Let this love be a completely devouring flame of God's love for God. Let all this be uprooted from me, devoured by God, transformed into the substance of Christ and given to eat to sufferers who lack all forms of nourishment in soul and body. And let me be paralyzed, blind, deaf, witless, and senile. (*CS* 204–5)

Nevin finds Weil "in covert rivalry with God here because God himself can be present to humanity only in a piece of matter" (287); indeed, the desire for illumination seems absent, and Weil returns to the image of the ruined self, still her preoccupation, its subsistence now a corollary of the eucharistic transformation. Her imagination stops short of contemplating death, perhaps in keeping with the psychological mechanism detected in her work by Oxenhandler:

The theme of mastery is in a condition of binary opposition with contrasting themes of renunciation, abjection, suffering, and "decreation." ... [T]he emotional tone of her work ... involves a tension between opposing impulses toward mastery and abjection. Here, abjection takes the form of a disbelief in her own reality, accounting for her indifference to death. If she was not really alive, she couldn't die. (186–87)

The structure of the prayer mirrors exactly a binary opposition of forces, and the survival of the afflicted "I" is perhaps projected out of that abjection. Weil's enumeration of mental and physical powers seems to have much less to do with the subject of mortification of the appetites than with questions of absolute possession and control. At the same time, the breakdown of logic suggested by the apparently false start of the prayer, along with the speaker's wish for an imperfectly accomplished annihilation, may also confirm the tentativeness, the uneasiness of the exploration. What is this vegetative state she seems to implore? The condition of paralysis, something suffered by her friend Joë Bousquet, wounded in the Great War, seems to represent for Weil a threshold to truth and rationale for recklessness; she calls for it here, and it is Bousquet's approval she cites in introducing her proposal to send nurses to the Allied front lines, certain to undergo a terrible death. She seems to be testing the limits of self-possession; once it has been relinquished, what shall we be? In this prayer, a residue of the person survives; there is neither complete sublimation nor complete erasure. The suspension of the self in what is neither fully life, nor fully death speaks to the imagination, as does the final scene of Balzac's *Le Colonel Chabert*, a work with which Weil was quite familiar (*VSW* 361–62), in which the egregiously wronged hero is glimpsed, destroyed in his old age, at the insane asylum of Charenton. Upon completion of the exercise, Weil admits that she understands nothing about "these spiritual phenomena" (205), again consigning it to the status of an experimental text, at a remove from experience.

To call down a horrible fate with such linguistic precision may be a way of keeping it firmly at arm's length, inscribing on the page what one cannot want to believe might be inscribed on the body; the cool manipulation of language in the first part of the prayer calls to mind nothing so much as the minute description of the torture apparatus in Kafka's story, "In the Penal Colony." But the revision constituted by the second part shows the beginning not to have been fully controlled or achieved with respect to its stated ends. The intensity, even avidity of the wish to be stricken is consonant with Weil's notorious remark: "[E]ach time I think of the crucifixion of Christ, I commit the sin of envy" (*AD* 62). While it is a variation on the theme she borrows from the Christian mystics, her prayer is not merely an exercise in theory; emotion and imagination are involved, the risk of self-exposure met bravely. Perhaps Weil drew inspiration from Pascal's "Prayer Asking God the Right Use of Illness" (605–14)—almost certainly the source of the title of her essay "Reflections on the Right Use of School Studies in View of Love for God" (*AD* 85–97)—which is more overtly a plea for rescue:

> To whom will I cry out, Lord, to whom will I have recourse if not to you? Everything that is not God cannot fulfill my expectation. It is God himself I implore and I seek; it is to you alone, my God, that I address myself in order to obtain you. Open my heart, Lord; enter into that rebellious place vices have occupied. They hold it in subjection; enter into it as into the strong man's house; but first tie up the strong and powerful enemy who controls it, and then take its treasures. (608)

Pascal's plea anticipates response; the "I" cries out, always and exclusively to "you," the addressee of the petition being made quite clear. God will actively take possession of the speaker's heart ("open . . . enter . . . tie up . . . take"), and his intervention is actively sought ("I implore . . . I seek . . . I address myself"). He will reassert his mastery, storming the heart like a medieval lord whose stronghold has been usurped. Weil's speaker shares with Pascal the qualities of absolutism and impatience; her speaker, too, is wholly uninterested in anything beyond the petition and resolutely implores. But whereas Pascal reacts to danger, Weil specifies no emergency and postulates an utter stasis, translated by her use of the passive voice and the verb "to be" generally. Pascal questions, asserts, importunes, sends a bulletin; his language is urgent and fluent, full of imagery, varied in structure. In Weil, the *fiat* is unvarying in structure ("That I might be beyond any condition . . . That I might be incapable," etc.); the similes occur predictably, stripped of the element of surprise ("like a total paralytic . . . like someone totally blind," etc.). No subtlety accompanies the evocation of extreme debilitation ("total," "completely"). Pascal depicts a battle; Weil's speaker is wholly oppressed.

Pascal's fervor rightfully belongs in a heart eager to house a personal God, but the fires burning in Europe during Weil's lifetime were of another kind. When she wrote these words in "La Personne et le sacré," she was referring to no abstraction:

If someone recognizes the reality of misfortune, he must tell himself: "A play of circumstances I don't control can take anything away from me at any instant, including all those things that are so much mine that I consider them as being myself. There is nothing in me that I might not lose. An accident can at any time abolish what I am and put in its place any vile and contemptible thing whatsoever."
To think that with the whole soul is to experience nothingness. (*EL* 35)

That Weil's imagination should so readily, so coldbloodedly evoke the devastation of the self in place of sensory mortification when she writes in imitation of the mystics' prayer cannot wholly surprise us, coming upon her work with an awareness of the Nazi era.

That she, unlike Pascal, does not anticipate rescue must likewise strike us as realistic. It is this tone of steely prophecy that justifies Patrick McCarthy's assessment: "She is hard on the Old Testament and its theme of a chosen people, but in her uncompromising rejection of power and her determination to turn affliction into a value one may see a response, however oblique, to the plight of the European Jews in the 1940s" (747). It is, of course, the obliqueness of that response that has so often caused it to be called into question. In so many things, as Milosz says of her, "Simone Weil was courageous. If she considered something true, she would say it, without fear of being labeled" (56). But the lacuna continues to disturb us; the rare note of outrage (*EL* 68) amid all the evidence of great personal anguish leaves the reader at a loss to comprehend.

In the "example of prayer" and "La Personne et le sacré," one narrative strand boldly approaching the shattering contemporary reality of Hitler's war visibly collides with the narrative inherited from Pascal; a wrenching psychological portrait of the individual on the brink of annihilation is given over to the dominant religious discourse, as if the only frame. Clearly, the integrity of Weil's Christian belief required her to tell the truth as she saw it and in the language she had made her own, that of the seventeenth-century French writers, as she wrote to the Minister of Education in 1940 protesting her expulsion from the teaching profession (*VSW* 528). That her indictment of an anti-Semitic statute occasioned a protest of her distance from her Jewish heritage may indicate only that hers was initially an inadequate response to the full dimensions of the enormity beginning to unfold—if, as Weil says, the inexpressible must be truly inexpressible, then the incomprehensible must be truly incomprehensible—but that Weil's discourse remained exclusive, shutting Judaism out, is painful to consider now and was no doubt part of her personal tragedy. Her commitment to winning the war against Germany, with all the horrors she dared to contemplate, was complete. How else but in light of this paradox is one to consider these words from a notebook she kept in London:

> Gather the people behind Christian aspirations. . . . It is necessary to try to define them in terms to which an atheist can wholly adhere, and in a way removing none of their specificity. That is quite possible. . . . What should be done is to propose

something precise, specific, and acceptable for Catholics, Protestants, and atheists—not as a compromise, but . . . —and immediately ask resistance and especially syndicalist groups whether that is their orientation. . . . Even a professed Christian needs this translation—because we think in profane terms—required to break down the impenetrable barrier not only between men, but with the soul. (*EL* 169–70).

"[N]ot as a compromise, but . . . ": Weil advocates the identification of words that transcend religious, political, and economic divisions, that overcome disbelief, that shatter obstacles to social and inner harmony. But her own language, upon inspection, proves not to be universal, sometimes even working to the benefit of a "we" delimited in an oppressive way. Perhaps we can recognize this "acceptably" defined imperative, born of historical emergency, as a misguided dream. "La Personne et le sacré" and "Prologue," Weil's parable of a mystical encounter possibly influenced by Baudelaire, are visibly efforts to achieve this translation of religious inspiration into worldly terms. Yet in at least one instance when Weil's imagination turns openly to Christian forms, as in her example of mystical prayer derived from John of the Cross, it finds no place for her, only the prospect of devastation. Realism takes many forms. Language cannot undo the reality of injustice; but if it is not to be complicit, it cannot let criminal silencing be passed over in silence. The impetus for the prayer—the unbearable protest of "[t]hat deep, childlike part of the heart that always anticipates the good" (*EL* 13)—remains trapped in the "I"—frozen in fear or horror, perhaps, and stubbornly resistant to the translation Weil is not able in the end to provide, one to an appropriate religious setting or a collective context acknowledging the suffering of the Jewish people.

3

"Prologue"

A painter doesn't draw the place where he himself is. But looking at his painting, I know his position in relation to the things he has drawn. On the contrary, if he represents himself in his painting, I know with certainty that the place he shows himself to be isn't the one where he is. (*CS* 97–98)

Reading "La Personne et le sacré" and the exercise in prayer, one enters abruptly into their creator's thought. We are left to deduce, if we can, the starting point for such works; with the confidence that she is only transposing absolute truths, Weil dispenses with many of the formalities of writing some find necessary, or at least hospitable, forms of recognition of the reader's presence. Part of the disorientation one may experience when reading her later works springs precisely from the sense that the texts are uninhabitable. There is no room for argument. One assents or one does not. One climbs to her point of elevation or, remaining below, one accepts her teachings; it is impossible to stay on one's own terms. This absence of accommodation makes her works seem more objectlike, as if flung unceremoniously at the mind below for the grasping. Intellectually speaking, this sovereign defiance is an effective challenge. One is reminded of Weil's great amusement upon receiving a letter from a reader of one of her articles asking, plaintively, "Madame ... *who* are you?" (*VSW* 533). Flannery

O'Connor's instinct to hunt for a photograph was not totally without precedent.

Thus it is intriguing to come to Weil's "Prologue," copied into a notebook from 1942 with the words, "Beginning of the book (the book containing these thoughts and many others)," and followed by the notation: "There follows an unorganized mass of fragments" (C 3:291–92). As if a rare gesture to the reader, the "Prologue," a brief allegory of a mystical encounter, is presumably to serve as compass or key. In Weil's projected book, whose form brings Pascal's *Pensées* immediately to mind, the illusion of wholeness is shattered; if Dickinson can say, "when I try to organize—my little Force explodes" (2:414), Weil indicates that her work, past rescue of narrative, has already exploded. Attuned to the temper of the modern era, her projected book of fragments will take its place beside similarly conceived works of Rilke, Pessoa, and Borges; in his discerning reading of its opening statement, Oxenhandler shows the closeness in spirit of the "Prologue" to Kafka's parables as well, along with its direct indebtedness to George Herbert's poem "Love" (194–99).

The poetic character of the "Prologue" and its intended association with a prose work freed of conventional narrative constraints suggest also literary descent from that strange modernist work "with neither head nor tail" (1:275), made in the image of a serpent, and performing "the miracle of a poetic prose, musical though without rhyme or meter, supple and accented enough to adapt to the soul's lyrical movements, the undulations of reverie, the sudden jolts of conscience" (1:275–76): Baudelaire's collection of prose poems, *Le Spleen de Paris* (1869). The portrait of modern urban life that emerges from its kaleidoscopic pages is not without relation to familiar moral and metaphysical territory:

> "Nearly all our troubles come to us from not having known how to stay in our room," said another sage, Pascal, I think, thereby calling to mind in the cell of recollection all those crazed people who seek happiness in movement and in a prostitution I might call *fraternal*, if I wanted to use the fine language of my century. (1:314)

Given her vast culture, Weil surely would have known the prose poems of the great innovator in the genre, just as she was fully familiar with the works of Rimbaud, to whom she addressed an unpublished poem (Nevin 165–67), and Mallarmé, whom she honored with the epithet, "a true poet" (*E* 297), also early practitioners of the form. Her "Prologue" shares with Baudelaire's work the solitary figure in a room as point of departure, the sense of fallenness and aloneness to be overcome in the busy Parisian streets, and the intuition of an intimate connection between the two settings, though seen in the different lights of the sure knowledge of evil (Baudelaire's explicitly serpentine creation) and the astonishing knowledge of the divine (Weil's mystical certainty). If the linguistic virtuosity of Baudelaire's narrator, who can pick and choose among varieties of speech, stands in stark contrast to Weil's prose starved of modulation and adornment, both kinds of rhetoric are equally the product of control. If the narrator in Baudelaire is loquacious and sociable, it is all the better to ensnare us in the corrupting web we hypocritically ignore; Weil's initiate is wholly engaged in the experience, requiring not our complicity but rather our acknowledgment of a truth beyond ourselves. Baudelaire's point of reference is the self-knowledge hidden in our hearts; Weil's is that reality on the other side of the sky. To compare the two writers, incongruous as the effort may seem, is to gain a sense of the prose poem as a field containing precariously within its bounds competing moral and aesthetic forces.

Having left Paris in the wake of the French military defeat in June 1940, Weil composed her allegory of spatial and temporal uprootedness in Marseilles:

> He entered my room and said, "You miserable creature, you who understand nothing and know nothing. Come with me and I'll teach you things you have no inkling of." I followed him.
>
> He led me into a church. It was new and ugly. He brought me before the altar and said, "Kneel down." I said to him, "I haven't been baptized." He told me, "Fall down on your knees before this place with love, as before the place where the truth is to be found." I obeyed. (*C* 3:291)

Without warning, without introduction, the divine teacher disrupts the privacy of the person sitting quietly in his own room, a cell not of recollection but of utter ignorance: this is Weil's frame for the mystical initiation. Along with his peremptoriness in general, bold-ness in speech characterizes the intruder, an attitude not automati-cally granted in Weil's symbolic universe (consider the beggar before Talleyrand, the tramp before the judge, the tongueless victim at-tempting to speak); such authority is usually instead her own pre-rogative as narrator (the castigation of human frailty from on high, the prayer tempting the Almighty to destroy his creation). Here, as in "La Personne et le sacré," with its "village idiot" (EL 31), and the prayer, with its plea to destroy the mind, the intellect is singled out for metaphorical assault. Claiming ascendance over the narrator's intelligence, the Christ figure promises a new kind of truth and language to express it, no doubt a representation of the evolution implicit in her later works where, as Florence de Lussy has observed, "[S]oon the whole domain of her reflection . . . is taken over by this mode of thought and writing" (426)—that is to say, mysticism.

The irruption of a supernatural force into ordinary space and time does not entirely disconcert the reader of Poe or Baudelaire familiar with such intrusions. According to Walter Benjamin, "Baudelaire placed the shock experience at the very center of his artistic work. . . . [He] made it his business to parry the shocks, no matter where they might come from, with his spiritual and his physical self. This shock defense is depicted graphically in an atti-tude of combat" (163). The response of Weil's narrator contrasts sharply with the often violent one found in Baudelaire whenever an uncontrollable impulse or event invades the consciousness and threatens its equilibrium, ever precarious. In "Le Mauvais vitrier" ("The Wicked Glazier"), the narrator, whose first mistake it is to have opened his window, is seized by a feeling of hatred "as sud-den as it was despotic" (1:286) and invites the unsuspecting glassmaker upstairs only to subject him to ridicule. Similarly, the bored narrator of "Assommons les pauvres!" ("Let's beat up the poor!") obeys an inner prompting to attack a beggar (1:357–59). The demonic character of the impulse, the substitution of aesthetic cri-teria for ethical ones in making judgments (the glassmaker is found deficient in his art, hence deserving of harassment), the aggressive language—all of these attempts to meet violence with violence will do nothing to relieve the narrator of his essential solitude and vul-nerability to suggestion (something well understood by the speaker in "La Solitude" [1:313]).

In Weil's "Prologue" there is an automatic quality to the narrator's actions; he follows, he obeys. When commanded to kneel, he demurs, not on the grounds of unbelief, but on ritualistic ones, firmly ignored by the imperious guide who merely rephrases his command. The transfer of setting from the narrator's room to the nondescript modern church does not alter the private nature of the encounter. Dislocation and genuflection symbolically contradict the attitude of self-possession implicit in the narrator's original withdrawal; the self must be ushered to the truth. The divine figure actually controls the seemingly arbitrary sequence of events.

The mention of baptism draws attention to itself on at least two counts; in this narrative, it is at first cited as an obstacle to revelation and then will be shown emphatically not to be one. If the choice of a Christian setting dictates the terms of the implied opposition—either one has been baptized or one has not—only to set it aside, one senses in this the effort, described in the note from London, to find that common language appealing to Christian and atheist alike. The dominant spirit—that love in the name of which the narrator is ordered to kneel—reigns supreme; if the "Prologue" is to contain a compass needle pointing to the truth, it is one magnetized by a compelling Christian belief. In Weil's parable, acceptance of these terms seems to entail the compulsory abandonment of an unaffiliated, or otherwise affiliated, state: her narrator's immediate reaction to the new setting is seen to reflect feelings of non-belonging or exclusion. Another level of anxiety and alienation is implicit in the word *"baptisé"* (baptized), in the masculine form in the French; once more, a notion of universality that tends to exclude rather than embrace appears to be at work. But whereas, in this symbolic universe oriented to Christian values, an attitude of love is shown to triumph over the unadministered sacrament, the feminine simply disappears. Access to higher knowledge is represented as a male province.

The word *"baptisé"* standing at the crossroads of these contradictions, the theme of dominance lends its harsh edge to the portrayal of the individual's relation to God, a brutality visible also in the internal dynamics of "the terrible prayer." Nevin's view of Weil's Christ as "one conjured up in bewilderment and anger over the loneliness of humankind on earth" (278)—that is, one reflecting her personal predicament and the general shock in the wake of contemporary events—rejoins Oxenhandler's analysis of the text as a modernist allegory in which "[a]rbitrary behavior disconnects action from psychology, pointing to the absurd character of life and the contingent nature of experience" (198–99). Self-determination is revealed as an illusion on more than one plane.

If there is a more than superficial resemblance between the shock experience represented in Baudelaire and the mystical experience portrayed by Weil—both writers registering in their prose the effects of a violent exposure to compelling forces originating deep within the psyche—this affinity may perhaps be located in the moral dimension underlying their depictions of the Parisian setting, a setting that compounds the feeling of powerlessness in the individual. Benjamin observes that the person wandering the city streets, the *flâneur*, whose sensitivity is constantly jolted by contact with the crowd, has an experience akin to that of unskilled workers in factories. Baudelaire himself "did not have the faintest notion of [industrial work processes]. He was, however, captivated by a process whereby the reflecting mechanism which the machine sets off in the workman can be studied closely, as in a mirror, in the idler" (177). Benjamin goes on to compare the activity of the gambler, a familiar figure in *Le Spleen de Paris*, with that of the worker: "[I]t certainly does not lack the futility, the emptiness, the inability to complete something which is inherent in the activity of a wage slave in the factory. . . . The work of both is equally devoid of substance" (177). The intolerable conditions of factory labor, against which Weil reacted early on, themselves become the stuff of consciousness, destroying the capacity to reflect beyond them. Intellectual and artistic creation, requiring quiet, introspection, and craft, is the antithesis of such work. Baudelaire's sympathy for the gambler and the other misfits he portrays and Weil's activism in behalf of the syndicalist movement are, in their different ways, direct responses to the oppressiveness of modern urban life.

Weil claimed that her factory experience left her with the indelible impression of having been marked a slave (*AD* 42); that this ordeal was present in her thoughts as she composed the "Prologue" is confirmed by her mother's note that the church "must be the one she speaks of [in] *La Condition ouvrière*, located near the factory where she was working" (ms. Bibliothèque Nationale de France). The unexplained docility of the narrator of the "Prologue" would certainly be consistent with a modern servitude that is meant to ensure intellectual exhaustion. The dispersal of energies, physical and spiritual, has a narcotic effect on the masses in the devouring, vacuous core of society—the capital, the head, seat of spirit and intellect—that is industrialized Paris. In such an atmosphere, already memorably evoked by Balzac in *La Fille aux yeux d'or* (1835), surely a source for Baudelaire, the notion of an impenetrable "cell of recollection" is suspect; there is no licit escape from the pervasive stepped-up rhythms of city life, the fluid movement of the crowd, or the urge to consume. Modern technology has sealed off the abyss Pascal, in his terror, proclaimed; now it is our shallowness that quite literally drives us to distraction. If it is true that Weil's narrator cannot resist the visitor's summons to go out any more than Baudelaire's can manage to stay away from windows, still she represents the motivating force as the desire for a teaching, not just a craving to fill up emptiness. Her narrator's submissiveness corresponds to her concept of obedience: "The best life possible has always seemed to me one in which everything is determined either by the constraint of circumstances or by such impulses [related to one's personal vocation] and where there is never any room for choice" (*AD* 38).

Baudelaire's "Le Joueur généreux" ("The Generous Gambler"), luxuriant in its prose, Satanic in its theme, allows us to see what Weil's "Prologue" is not:

> Yesterday, passing through the crowd on the boulevard, I felt myself brushed up against by a mysterious Being whom I had always desired to know and whom I recognized at once, although I had never seen him before. There must have been an analogous desire toward me on his part, for as he passed by he gave me a meaningful wink of the eye I hastened to obey. I followed him carefully, and soon I went down after him into a dazzling underground abode resplendent with luxury none of the dwellings above in Paris could remotely approach. It struck me as odd that I could have passed by this prestigious haunt so often and never have noticed the entrance. (1:325)

The uncanny moment occurs when the narrator is out among the crowd, which produces the shock (being "brushed up against") that generates the poem. Nameless but instinctively recognized, like Weil's "He," the "mysterious Being" seems to have the specific mission of accosting the speaker and introducing him to an unfamiliar site all too easily overlooked—here, the opulent den, as opposed to the bare, unremarkable church. Infinitely more voluble and accommodating than Weil's narrator, the *flâneur* immediately opens up a space of psychological commerce—the projection of corresponding desires to know each other on the part of the characters—unavailable in the master-slave relationship between God and the self as imagined by Weil. Something similar transpires in the tacit exchange between reader and narrator; Baudelaire's speaker assumes we want to be approached and provides familiar signposts from daily life ("Yesterday," "the boulevard," the chance meeting, the unnoticed entryway). There is nothing spartan about the prose, and the attraction to luxury and subterranean hideaways is resolutely un-Weilian (it was the three-year-old Simone who refused a pretty ring, saying, "I don't like luxury" [*VSW* 18]). An encounter with the Devil is more entertaining than Christ's austere visitation, but entertainment is the low road, and Weil's aspiration toward a universal language the high one. The reader is put on trial.

Time and space receive more ample attention in the continuation of Weil's allegory:

> He made me go out and then climb up to an attic with an open window from which one could see the whole city, wooden scaffolding, the river where boats were being unloaded. Inside the attic were only a table and two chairs. He made me sit down.
>
> We were alone. He spoke. Once in a while somebody would come in, join in the conversation, and then leave.
>
> It was no longer winter. It wasn't yet springtime. The tree branches were bare, without buds, out in the cold and sun.
>
> Daylight would climb, dazzle, and fade, and then moon- and starlight would come in through the window. Then once again the morning sun would rise. (*C* 391–92)

Although details are deliberately kept to a minimum, the setting is indeed Paris, the Paris of Weil's factory year (1934–35) joined with the Paris of her mystical experiences (from 1938 on), often occurring while she was reciting Herbert's poem "Love" in the midst of

migraine headaches (*AD* 44–45). It is the city that variously orches-
trates the annihilation of the intellect through physical pain, the one
kind of experience leaving the self crushed, the other leading to
transcendence; in both cases, the violent assault on the senses forces
upon the individual a spiritual leavetaking of the body, a sense of
otherness. The representation of Paris, Weil's native city, suddenly
in June 1940 no longer hers, comes freighted with associations of
foreignness, the alienation of factory work now linked symbolically
with the sense of exclusion felt inside a church, the recitation of a
poem in English, and the mystical visitation itself, unlike any other
experience. Roles are reversed; now the narrator is the guest in his
teacher's room. Boundaries are blurred, permeable; the figures are
alone, and sometimes a third person is present; the season is suspended between winter and spring. Time is cyclical, unending. The
attic is porous, absorbing light, allowing visitors to come and go,
opening a perspective on nature, architecture, and people at work.
More specifically, the window is like an open book, the trees, stars,
and sun so many symbols to be read, an approach to the physical
world J. P. Little calls "at once practically medieval and very distinctive" (52), unique to Weil. Miraculously, there is conversation.
In poverty and displacement, there is a kind of elevation, one a
world apart from Baudelaire's treatment of this theme. Weil's text
continues:

> Occasionally he would grow silent and take a loaf of bread
> from the shelf, and we would share it. That bread truly had the
> taste of bread. I have never found that taste since.
> He would pour out for both of us wine that tasted of the
> sun and earth where the city had been built.
> Sometimes we would stretch out on the attic floor, and the
> sweetness of sleep would come over me. Then I would wake
> up again and drink in the sunlight.
> He had promised me a teaching, but he didn't teach me at
> all. We talked about all kinds of things, in no particular fashion,
> like old friends. (*C* 3:292)

In this scene of an informal communion, restating with images
taken from nature the Christian context expressed in the architecture of the working people's church, Weil's narrative asserts that

initiation to mystical knowledge, of a kind far surpassing the mere teachings of the intellect, does not depend on formal signs of conversion. It is shown the superior sacrament, seemingly transcending the issue of belonging or not belonging through baptism and incorporating in their fullness the fruits of nature. But sexual desire, its presence hinted at transparently, is not integrated into the new order established here. The narrator himself, now unable to replace that unforgettable bread, is not definitively admitted to this attic paradise, either. According to Oxenhandler, "Weil's text deals with her lifelong desires for meaning and for love and the frustration of those desires in a meaningless world" (199). The ambiguity of inclusion or exclusion with respect to a given order remains a preoccupation, an underlying geological fault over which the interlude of happiness is imperfectly suspended. Unsurprisingly, Weil's extremism is implicit in the terms of the visit: either one lives the eucharistic moment, or one loses it irretrievably. If Pascal can say that, "without the hunger for spiritual things, one grows weary of them" (1155), Weil admits only of the hunger. The things of the spirit are not mere possessions, easily within our grasp. They do not belong to us any more than we ourselves belong in their presence.

If mystical union surpasses the power of the intellect to comprehend and express it, the scene described here is necessarily that rare instance of fiction in Weil's work, in this case the attempted metaphorical transposition of something by definition ineffable. The willed simplicity of Weil's language, at times almost painful to read— the impoverished vocabulary, the extreme deliberateness of the description of each gesture—speaks more of determination than felicity. Perhaps this is the moment she is painting herself into her picture, at odds with the limitations of language and the imagination; with more certainty, one can say that her imagination has a didactic cast, inhibiting full flight in a poetic setting. In her notebooks and essays, by way of contrast, she draws on a wide range of experience to provide illustrations that surprise, illuminate, and often delight, and she does so with consummate ease and authority. One need only think of the many apt and startling images in "La Personne et le sacré."

In "Le Joueur généreux," the Satanic parallel to the communion scene runs nearly complete:

My host and I were already, as we sat down, grand old friends.
We ate, we drank to excess all kinds of extraordinary wines. . . . I
must say that [in the course of the evening] I had gambled and
lost my soul, hand in glove [with my host], with heroic light-
ness of spirit and insouciance. . . .

We smoked unhurriedly a few cigars whose incomparable
taste and odor awoke in the spirit a nostalgia for unknown
lands and pleasures. . . .

We also talked of the universe, of its creation and its future destruction, and of the great idea of the century, that is to
say, progress and perfectibility. . . . His Highness . . . spoke with
a smoothness of diction and an evenness of humor that I have
found in none of humanity's most celebrated conversational-
ists. He explained to me the absurdity of the different philoso-
phies that had up until now taken possession of the human
brain.

Encouraged by so much kindness, I asked him news of God
and whether he had seen him lately. (1:326–27)

The narrator has followed the Devil underground into the gam-
bling parlor, where other lost souls, a ghostly counterpart of the
crowd on the boulevard, are in attendance. Perfect civility reigns.
Satan is an exemplary host; food and wine are served and con-
sumed in abundance; cigars taste not of the city or region, but of
unfulfilled desires, of lands unknown. Sensuality and corruption
are right at home here. The loss of one's soul, casually mentioned,
in no way disrupts the proceedings. Like the corresponding figures
in Weil's allegory, the narrator and the Devil seem old friends; the
conversation flows freely, touching on "all kinds of things." By way
of critique, Weil's narrator observes that his host fails to teach him
anything; Baudelaire's appreciates the Devil's seductive eloquence.
The austere style of the one work contrasts with the dense, expansive style of the other. The Devil expounds in particular on the
notion of progress, one Weil wholeheartedly abhorred; images of
the cycles of nature and the earth's unchanging relation to sun and
stars are her answer to that modern plague, which the Devil also
finds risible. Weil's "Prologue" almost seems a gloss on Baudelaire's
poem, as if taking up the challenge of the gambler's inquiry after
God himself.

The festivities draw to a close:

> At last, as the chilly dawn was frosting the window panes, this
> celebrated person . . . told me: "I want you to have a good
> memory of me. . . . In order to compensate the irremediable loss
> of your soul, I am giving you the stakes you would have won
> if fate had worked in your favor, that is to say, the possibility
> to relieve and conquer, your whole life long, that bizarre ail-
> ment of Ennui, source of all your maladies and your wretched
> progress." . . .
>
> If it had not been for the fear of humbling myself in front
> of so large an assembly, I would gladly have fallen at the feet
> of this generous gambler, thanking him for his unheard-of
> munificence. But gradually, after I had left him, an incurable
> mistrust returned to my breast; I no longer dared believe in
> such miraculous fortune, and, upon going to bed, saying my
> prayers out of a vestige of idiotic habit, I repeated to myself in
> my demi-slumber: "My God! Lord, my God! Make the devil
> keep his word!" (1:327–28)

Whereas Weil's narrator, refreshed by sleep, wakes to drink in the
morning light as it pours through an open window, Baudelaire's
speaker has but one night of companionship; heedful of the hour,
he makes motions to leave. Here, the first light plays on panes of
glass; it is known through indirection only; its coolness gives no
indication of the season. Although the narrator has gambled and
lost, his gracious host offers him a permanent consolation. Aware of
the public setting, the gambler suppresses an effusive gesture of
thanks; back in his room, however, he finds the Devil's generosity
suspect and, reflexively and comically, calls on God to intercede in
his behalf.

The "Prologue" ends more abruptly and with a different kind
of ambiguity:

> One day he told me, "Go away now." I fell to my knees, I flung
> my arms around his legs, I begged him not to chase me away.
> But he threw me out on the stairs. I went downstairs stunned,
> my heart shattered. I walked around in the streets. Then I real-
> ized I had no idea where that house was.

I have never tried to find it again. I understood that he had only come to get me by mistake. My place is not in that attic. It is anywhere at all, in a prison cell, in one of those bourgeois parlors full of red plush and bibelots, in the waiting room of a train station, anywhere at all—but not in that attic.

I can't keep myself from repeating sometimes, with fear and remorse, some of what he told me. How can I be sure of remembering exactly? He isn't here to tell me.

I know quite well that he doesn't love me. How could he love me? And yet something deep within, a particle of myself, can't help thinking, all the while trembling with fear, that perhaps, in spite of everything, he does love me. (C 3:292)

Unashamed to make the supplicating gesture Baudelaire's gambler circumspectly avoids, Weil's narrator is forced out on the street, back among the gamblers and factory workers who fill their lives with meaningless gestures, whether insincere prayers or the routine of piecework, and who provide the poet what might be from the initiate's point of view more instances of the same, those art-giving shocks that dare to consort with evil. Nevin calls Weil's Christ figure "a cad and a bully" and wonders, "Why should she want this creature to love her?" (277). His reading of the text centers on Weil's trepidation before the prospect of conversion to Roman Catholicism, culminating in a sense of being an outcast; her sense of exclusion is at once the impetus for "an involuntary *imitatio Christi*" (277) and a reflex consistent with the brutal political realities of Vichy France. To this one must add Weil's familiarity with the writings of the Christian mystics; in John of the Cross, the dark night of the soul precedes mystical rapture—Weil reverses the order—but is expressed in similar terms: "This sensory and spiritual peace, since it is still imperfect, must first be purged; the soul's peace must be disturbed and taken away. . . . [the mystical seeker] suspects that he is lost and that his blessings are gone forever" (348). As in her prayer, an edge of violence characterizes the representation of spiritual loss.

If the rejection of the narrator seems as arbitrary and inexplicable as the summons he first obeys, the parable itself unfolds in a manner reminiscent of "Le Joueur généreux," as if a narrative logic held sway. The warmth of intimacy gives way to the chill of solitude, with the accent on culture and hypocrisy on the one hand,

and simplicity and brutality on the other. After the moment of parting, the gambler goes up to the street and home to his attic room; Weil's narrator goes down to the street and discovers he is homeless. One doubts the cure of malaise his supernatural companion promised him; the other doubts his own memory of, and his acceptability to, the Other. One invokes God in an effort to prolong the illusion of well-being; the other knows the ecstatic moment cannot be regained. If the plot lines are similar, one fundamental difference on the level of theme clearly emerges: the gambler, who knowingly puts his soul at risk, cannot honestly say that the Devil cheated him; from Weil's parable of unwitting subjection to abrupt gain and loss comes the bitter knowledge that we have no firm roots on earth or in heaven. Against this injustice on the human and cosmic scales, we can only oppose a particle of hope.

Unlike Baudelaire's seamless tale, Weil's allegory seems to founder, breaking off into a psychological confession of unworthiness. Within the text there is an air of irresolution; in Oxenhandler's words, the work "approaches meaning asymptotically, without ever achieving full clarity" (196). It is as if the ambition to speak of transcendence itself is rudely rebuffed, the narrative suddenly confined to a lower plane. Expulsion applies not only to the narrator, but to language in its fractured contact with the inexpressible. However limpid Weil's style, the "Prologue" lacks the power of evocation and authority one might hope to find in a fully achieved prose poem; that is not to question the authenticity of her experience, but to acknowledge the difficulty of the task she set herself. But the breakdown is not a purely linguistic phenomenon, or rather, it is not possible to isolate the linguistic element to the exclusion of other factors. Among them, as Oxenhandler so convincingly demonstrates, is the inner conflict refracted in the urgent telling of the tale:

> Weil's conflicting drives are mirrored in the paradoxical behavior of her absent-present visitor, an angel or the Crucified One himself. Doubt, fear, remorse, those familiar emotional states, blot out the momentary experience of happiness. She writes it down feverishly, an inadequate record that conveys a factualness that can't be argued away. (199)

Indeed, in terms of poetic creation, the "Prologue" shows signs of the strain of the attempt to create, without also trusting to the free play of the imagination, an allegory based on private experience; no doubt the decision to put herself in the work, rather than stand back, made it difficult to achieve perspective. The extreme simplicity of style and sparseness of imagery also call to mind her ideal of a language capable of expressing Christian aspirations to the people of France (*EL* 169–70). The self-conscious attempt to renew Christian values and imagery, visible in the "Prologue" and in her later work in general, undertaken, as it was, in the era of the Occupation and Vichy France, raises the painful question of exclusion— Who exactly are the people of France, and who are not?—and is undermined by its claim to universality. Weil, who calls for new religious forms elsewhere, and who knows hers must be a book of fragments, could not singlehandedly create the perfect narrative or synthesize the many; as Miklos Vetö observes of her writings on aesthetics, "desire for the beautiful does not yet mean one is firmly established in the perspective of God, but in her moving descriptions, Weil is often forgetful of the difference" (96). Desiring the truth, one does not automatically transcend human limitations and history. Language brings us down to earth.

Reading the "Prologue," one cannot fail to be moved by the courage of the truth-seeker intent on leaving her book of thoughts behind, for what is the "Prologue" but a valedictory, a message in a bottle, as Mandelshtam might say, meant for a distant reader on a distant shore? Underlying Weil's parable of dispossession one senses a desperate will to fix what is broken, a will itself already doomed, shattered, or simply devoid of form, like the mass of fragments intended to follow. How can we abandoned in this world achieve wholeness? If the tapestry we weave out of our memories and illusions has been pulled out from under us, how are we to face the abyss about to devour us? If the moment of transcendence cannot even sustain the mystic, let alone those who have only the metaphor, what can the book, any book, with its teachings of the intellect, possibly bring us? What can this book written in shock and anguish and exile bring those excluded from the terms implied in its allegorical compass? Weil's tortured, denuded language, aspiring to be universal, breaks under the weight of its overwhelming burden. Perhaps her text is still saying, through all its points of rupture and silence and contradictory meaning, that works created in the "cell of recollection" can neither capture moments of ecstasy nor paper over abysses. Literature itself becomes a form of confinement, shutting itself off from those oppressed souls lost in the streets. It is not an adequate or convincing medium for the experience the writer wants to convey. Not surprisingly, then, "Prologue" is unique among Weil's writings. It is to her notebooks themselves that we must turn for the more compelling and inclusive record of both her spiritual quest and her engagement with the challenges of her era.

4

Notebooks

If the "Prologue" recounts a mystic's shattering experience of the meaninglessness and alienation of modern urban life, the notebooks Weil kept in Marseilles after the French collapse offer a different kind of reflection of the times: a response properly contained in words. The objects themselves, composed of small and now crumbling pages of cheap newsprint, convey something of the writing's character: its impromptu and, in a dark context, expendable nature; the identity of its substance with current events; the attempt to articulate things of value in the face of moral impoverishment; the scholar's simplicity, her eagerness to learn. Unlike other of Weil's writings, these are conceived as a series, a continuous investigation; they are not pronouncements from on high, but a form of discipline. By the time she ordered and numbered them and entrusted them to her friend Gustave Thibon, soon before her departure from France, Weil had outgrown them. Her detachment was complete.

The exploratory nature of journal writing, the liberty of not having to conceal motives (although Weil carefully makes no direct reference to work or colleagues in the Resistance circles she was associated with), the urgency taken on by the written word in a time when the very future of the language was imperiled—all of these allow for a freshness, an immediacy of insight and expression in the notebooks that so often invite from the reader a response similar to Flannery O'Connor's: "[I]f I really own the complete Simone Weil I feel very rich" (196). Whereas Weil's narratives speak almost uniformly of rejection and self-sacrifice, the notebooks define a habitable space, one made free for intellectual inquiry through trial and error; proclaiming the intrinsic value of the life of the mind, they seem to attest to the author's own resistance to some of the implications of her systematic *via negativa*. If Weil was to speak so disparagingly of her writing in London ("How could I not consider myself contemptible?" [*EL* 214]), the falseness she was reacting against was perhaps not only political in nature—the rejection of her proposal for the front-line nurses, the barrier to action externally imposed upon her—but also intellectual—the forced premise of her writing assignments, the very premature assumption, in 1942 and 1943, that the Allies would win the war. No such untoward assurance underlies the notebooks, which are very much of the moment (though in the spirit of Thoreau's injunction to attend not to the *Times*, but to the Eternities) and alive with the sense that everything is at risk.

A glance at these works—all that can be permitted within the small dimensions of this study—serves as a necessary reminder that, however singular Weil's voice and imagination, her works belong to the literature of an era, one in which writing and publication were inextricable from the poisoned atmosphere of collaboration, and in which writers faced judgment by their own pens each time they went to write. As previously noted, the content and presentation of Weil's essay "Expérience de la vie d'usine" (1942), for example, suffered from conditions imposed from both within (her revisions) and without (the editors' ancillary material) as it made the trajectory from the handwritten page into print. But such publication, in Weil's case, was rare. Although Weil had given some thought to preparing a book on her concept of reading, one for which she would have mined material in her notebooks (*OC* 6:1:409–11), she did not go about systematically altering the notes written in Marseilles as she had her factory journal. Ultimately she concluded that the indication of the light by which they should be read

("Prologue") was sufficient guide to the "mass of fragments" she was accumulating. The reader is left free to wander, as if among ruins. The shattering of form so preserved conveys the writer's sense of emergency, an inconclusiveness with respect to the future (if not on the moral plane), the refusal to be false, a resistance to pressure to conform. As Alice Kaplan notes, in the occupied countries of the Second World War, there was no escaping such pressure:

> When fascism took power, it took charge of the imaginary, using the most advanced sophisticated agents of representation available—cinema, radio, architecture, staged rallies—new elements in the "design" of everyday life that few knew to take seriously as political forces. It would be an error to describe fascist state media as an endlessly fascinating emotional coup. It was highly clichéd and boring, even to its devotees. But it was ubiquitous, and it had been prepared in several generations of higher brow art and literature. (34)

Weil's repeated avowal of the particular responsibility of writers in the catastrophe befallen Europe indicates her sense of the dishonesty of the narration of history according to the notion of progress, making of the present moment a necessary culmination; by presenting history as an inevitable sequence of events, the dimension of moral responsibility is dissolved. With the Nazi takeover, a new and terrible kind of propaganda displaces a hollow, and ultimately indefensible, nationalist ideology. Even in *L'Enracinement*, written on assignment in London, Weil insists on the provisional nature of any account of history, gathering, in the words of Christine Ann Evans, "data that might, *eventually*, form a narrative, but a narrative that will only be constituted *in the future*" ("The Nature of Narrative" 68); and in "Légitimité du gouvernement provisoire" (*EL* 58–73), she fearlessly reminds the Gaullists that there is nothing foreordained about their assuming political power after a military victory in France. If her vision for the future did not provide for a tabula rasa but was tied, as indicated by the organic metaphor, to a rural way of life that quickly vanished after the war, it also excluded the possibility of dismissing the French defeat as an aberration to be surmounted by mere chronology. This reality had to be confronted dispassionately.

Something similar was occurring in Weil's encounter with the brutally altered landscape she was forced to inhabit personally and intellectually. Although incapable of conceiving of a life for herself apart from her country, even as conditions of oppression in Vichy grew markedly worse (the Weils managed to leave France just before the law requiring Jews to wear the yellow star went into effect), Weil sought in her writing a space from which preconceptions—not unlike the prejudices unleashed with the Nazi victory—might be banished. It is as if she set out to test a belief that the crushing weight of the past and its terrible consequences might somehow be counterbalanced, if only in the moment, by the exercise of intellectual freedom in the act of writing. It is in the private writings of her notebooks—writings meant, if conditions warranted, to be glimpsed as if from over her shoulder, in the way a recorded piece of music or conversation might be overheard—that Weil fully rejoins, as a writer, the sphere of protest left to one side in some of her published writings and in the work required of her in London. Summarizing Arendt's remarks in *Between Past and Future* on the French Resistance, Jeffrey C. Isaac indicates the way in which the response of intellectuals opposed to the Occupation forces and Vichy—Camus and Char noteworthy among them—actually opened, unforeseen, a new public space:

> The heavy weight of moral responsibility was a form of liberation from "the weightless irrelevance of their personal affairs." Thus "without premonition and probably against their conscious inclinations, they had come to constitute willy-nilly a public realm where—without the paraphernalia of officialdom and hidden from the eyes of friend and foe—all relevant business in the affairs of the country was transacted in deed and word." . . . Ceasing to be suspicious of their own insincerity, they experienced themselves as authentic and free, "not, to be sure, because they acted against tyranny and things worse than tyranny—this was true for every soldier in the Allied armies—but because they had become 'challengers,' had taken the initiative upon themselves and therefore, without knowing or even noticing it, had begun to create the public space between themselves where freedom could appear." (34–35)

Freedom can also appear in the act of writing itself. In some of Weil's later work, when she is speaking to personal goals or experience, narrative itself—something connected with the preparation of work for publication—is like a form of tyranny leading to the symbolic exclusion of the speaker, as if replicating social and political forces surrounding her (the essay on factory experience, "Prologue," and her proposal). In the creation of her notebooks, Weil is required neither to impose an overarching line on the movement of her thought nor to represent herself personally as agent or character. Relieved of such constraints, her writing flows freely; as Le Dœuff observes, "it is hard to bear being in a situation where one is not allowed for a moment to forget what one is supposed to be. One might well be filled with a desire to be nothing, when every action is stifled by a coating of 'you are,' and always the same thing" (207). (Oxenhandler's allusion to Weil's struggle with interdiction [213] concerns specifically the notebooks written in New York, where her hopes of ever assuming some control over her response to the French catastrophe vanished.) As if signaling a recovery from the initial shock of displacement—the first entry dates from January 1941—the Marseilles notebooks begin with the fresh and energetic look of a "challenger," a role Weil had always relished, at the newly reconfigured landscape, at once home—a French city—and not home—neither the city of Paris nor free.

With the notebooks, Weil applies to her own unmediated experience the same impulses that inspired the journal of her factory year. As before, her point of departure would not be a given identity or ideology; the mind, unburdened by personal or communal history, would immerse itself in the rawness of new experience, confront the nature of its perceptions, and bring back a credible report. It will proceed at ground level, negotiating a minefield of evil and lies, dependent for the survival of its freedom on the correct reading of the signs all around it—a method in which the astonishing intuition of the essay on the *Iliad* rejoins the ordeal of daily experience as it has now become. The notebooks will make an intellectual use of the inescapable conditions at hand. That Weil opens her first Marseilles notebook with an epigraph from Aeschylus, translated by her elsewhere, "Through suffering, knowledge" (*OC* 6:1:455), indicates the trajectory; indeed, she might also have rewritten Descartes to read: "I suffer, therefore I know." She begins:

There are things that are not in themselves cause for any suffering, but that do cause suffering as *signs*. Signs of what? Of a state of things that *in itself* causes suffering only rarely (or *never?*), being too abstract in itself to constitute a misfortune. But the signs cause suffering from it, although not in themselves painful.

In this way: the defeat (cf. Gide's leaflets) and the sight of a German soldier in uniform.

Similarly, the identity card for Renault.

If such signs are frequent each day, there is misfortune.

Some things are in themselves causes of suffering. Physical suffering, in that case. Humiliation (it is a physical suffering).

Still others both in themselves and as signs. (Humiliation.) These are the most painful. (*OC* 6:1:220)

Weil's approach to the defeat seems mathematical, exploring the possible combinations of cause and effect in the act of perception. How, plunged into misfortune, does the mind grasp its situation? Not necessarily by its susceptibility to certain things, but to the piercing relation certain things may have to that mind's predicament. (Immersed in that predicament, the mind fails to grasp it fully.) The defeat, the far-reaching and specific consequences of which could only be imagined, as Gide had noted, with great difficulty (*OC* 6:1:476), becomes palpable in the perception of the inescapable strands of its web; the German soldier, the factory identification card, the insistent reality of humiliation allow the mind to perceive that it is caught in enslavement.

Weil studies the mental processes of the perceiving subject as if with scrupulous detachment, even as the source of her authority, her personal experience, remains transparent. This impersonal, microscopic examination of the mind in its immanency (perceptions, sensations, emotions, all open to interpretation) and in its contingency (vulnerability to circumstance and states of being) in effect makes of the subject an object, something concrete and real. A description of this process is exactly the one she interjects into the essay on factory experience in order to justify her claim to authority (in the passage "If someone having come from the outside..." discussed in the introduction [*OC* 2:2:300]); in the notebooks, no apology is required. For Weil, returning to her notebooks after a long hiatus, clearly this method is liberating, in keeping with the general experience outlined by Arendt; there is a strong sense of the mind's boundaries as it confronts so many hurtful obstacles, as well as a certain self-possession, manifest in its lucidity. The same sure sense of prowess in a given domain launches Char's poetic journal *Feuillets d'Hypnos*, a record of his year as a Resistance leader in the Basses-Alpes (1943–1944): "Insofar as possible, teach effectiveness for the sake of the goal at hand, but for nothing beyond that. Beyond that is smoke. Where there is smoke, there is change" (175).

Just as Char keeps below air made thick by smoke, so Weil deliberately seeks lucidity in the world of visible signs:

Problem: the defeat, not experienced as suffering at certain moments (fine day, beautiful landscape).

A man in a gray-green uniform is not the cause of suffering. (Example from before the hostilities, military attachés . . .)

The defeat having taken place, let a German soldier appear in the landscape, and suffering is born.

Pain originating in the link (of sign to signified) between two things not painful outside that link. And this pain can be felt in the body. (Can even cause tears.)

Is it the same for joy? Aesthetics, holidays . . . ? Ornaments for a holiday, for example. (*OC* 6:1:220)

Returning to her initial illustration, Weil's thought makes a circular motion; repetition (appearing also in her use of the word "humiliation," as if reinforcing its reality), accretion, persistence, parenthetical notations drawn from experience—these characteristics of her thought and language show us the difficulty of the topic, the way the emphases made are earned, and certainly the painfulness of progress, which omits no necessary step. The mind at first registers disparate objects of perception—the defeat is not a defeat, but the permanent landscape; the soldier is not a soldier, but a man wearing a certain color—and then the suspension of these is abolished, an internal operation. "The defeat having taken place," the irreducible contradiction appears, piercing the consciousness. To plot its location on this unsuspected plane, a new map is required. Although Weil does not speak in the first person, she is fully and openly implicated in the text, choosing to situate her thought and her physical presence ("this pain can be felt in the body") in terms of these coordinates for suffering. Transposed in impersonal terms, the equation defeats abstraction. Neither the defeat, nor the soldier, nor the speaker—all on French soil—can be removed from the geography, seen in its proper light (the birth of suffering); she will write later, " 'I suffer.' That is better than: 'This landscape is ugly' " (*OC* 6:2:291).

Weil's pictorial imagination, sketching a tableau, simplified but adequate to her purposes, is remarkably consistent; here, a foreign element (the German soldier) enters a landscape (a location in France) and brings into focus an otherwise imperceptible coloration (defeat), one also washing over the spectator ("Can even cause tears"). In her proposal for the front-line nurses, care-giving Allied women enter the battlefield dominated by the SS and make the moral dimension of the struggle visible to the public, who will be galvanized. Indeed, the proposal is an answer to the landscape of defeat, an alternate drawing prepared in advance; the plan had been uppermost in her mind even before the German offensive, and it is in a way appropriate that Weil should open her notebooks in Marseilles by defining the "problem" in terms of an image corresponding to it, one always presupposing her presence. Consistent also in a different register is the movement from the evocation of suffering to the evocation of joy with which the passage concludes; the psychological mechanism that has been so carefully dissected is itself a phenomenon, from this angle the context incidental. The present reality is not the only reality.

If Weil's "unerring instinct," in McLellan's words, "to go straight to the heart of the problems of our time" (2) leads her to study the mind's assimilation of terrible truths cast in a realistic setting, her poetic instinct as a writer inspires her to convey the violence of this introduction to a radically new perspective. If the prayer and the "Prologue" offer extreme examples of this dramatic sense, so also does this opening passage of the Marseilles notebooks, making of pain a necessary condition for correct seeing in what now passes for the most ordinary of circumstances. The primacy of relationship over object in the birth of suffering, implicitly contrasted with the birth of Christ recalled in the allusion to holiday festivities (still hollowly in the air, this January of 1941), brings the speaker's subjectivity to the fore and makes of it a conduit. Its susceptibility to this mechanism is revealed by the shock of the new situation; the general principle announced in the first lines of the text, like the military occupation they describe, proves to be no abstraction. Thus Weil chooses a theme—spiritual and physical violence—that coincides perfectly with her favored *modus operandi* in the notebooks at large: the propounding, in Evans's words, of "the carefully crafted gnomic statement that defies common wisdom, coupled with an example from everyday life presented as a minimal narrative situation, that together have the impact of a direct blow to the solar plexus" ("The Power of Parabolic Reversal" 314). An assault on the sensibilities of the reader is a small thing to administer when the future of a civilization is at risk. With the speaker we must wake to brute, unbearable reality.

Later in the notebooks, Weil formulates a general statement of the approach already adopted in the first entry:

War being an act upon the imagination, the first difficulty is to avoid the effect of imagination, to have at one's disposal (as for a problem in geometry) the various ways in which to combine the elements, the particulars. Allow a concrete situation to appear from another point of view. (Avoid the effect of unreality; *IN THE IMAGINARY, A SINGLE SYSTEM OF RELATIONS.*) (*OC* 6:1:303)

Oppression is reductive, forcing the single reading of signs (one is to think: the German soldier is in his rightful place); to remain freely in contact with reality, one must be prepared to read, to perceive relation, from the unexpected angle—one that will inevitably, in wartime, cause pain. Reading also requires an apprenticeship, if one is to be able to decipher the foreign-seeming characters thrust before our eyes: "A French woman receives a letter saying: *your son has been killed.* If she does not know English, the first sight of the letter has one effect on her. If she does know English, another effect (for example, fainting). Thus, through learning, we change the power sensations have to modify us" (*OC* 6:1:294). Once again, the informed reading implicates the reader and violently alters consciousness.

In exploring the bases for the necessary reorientation of thought after the upheaval of one's world, here caused by the French defeat, Weil begins to redefine and rebuild a world in which psychological mechanisms and, later, supernatural laws operate in a way that is compatible with physical reality. Introspection is not cut off from sensation; on the contrary, it is the thinking, feeling, perceiving human presence that animates the motionless backdrop lightly sketched by the indication of a soldier's presence or of a piece of paper covered with strange writing. The drama is interior, experienced mentally and physically. The mind does not intervene; that function is reserved for the proposal and for clandestine actions Weil could not consign to her notebooks for safety's sake. But the specific task of the intelligence is already a noble one: to brave the sight of unadorned reality, to restore a sense of right relation to the truth. Char, in his journal, says something similar: "Light has been driven from our sight. It is hidden somewhere in our bones. Now it is we who pursue it, in order to give it back its crown" (201). We can feel the truth in our bones and in our tears, these writers and patriots tell us, when it is not otherwise in evidence.

Weil, for whom the memory of her factory year had not faded ("Similarly, the identity card for Renault"), widens the scope of her inquiry:

> The relation of *I* and the world: I am this star [asterisk], in the way that, when I am writing, the barrel of the pen is part of my body, and in the way that, when I am pressing the bit of the drill on the metal, it is at their point of contact that my existence is located, and in the way that, when I am looking at a painting . . . and in other ways still. But the relation of *I* and other men [*sic*]? I am the one who sees the cube from this perspective, but also the one who sees it from that other [perspective] (from which I do not see it). I am the one who reads sensations according to this law, and the one who reads them according to that other law. (*OC* 6:1:295)

The self and the world exist in the present moment, the latter experienced as an extension of oriented effort. Weil puts writing, factory labor, and the appreciation of art under the same rubric—ways of being in the world—and so confirms, tacitly, her intention that these thoughts might someday be read. The poignancy of the example of the German soldier in the landscape resides precisely in the speaker's recognition that her existence is necessarily compatible with this spectacle; her world now extends to this. But the notion of extension does not apply in the sphere of human relations. Turning to yet another a mathematically inspired illustration, Weil simply states the fact of the existence of multiple points of view, an observation in keeping with the spirit of the notebooks, a declaration of intellectual independence. The self—any self—is singular in its subjectivity.

Weil's instinctive tolerance is, of course, part of the freedom missing from the earlier illustration. The soldier symbolizes the annihilating intent of an exclusive ideology; the speaker tastes the bitterness of that (still) subtle poison dispersed in the atmosphere, momentarily concentrated. While his foreignness is confirmed, along with the harmfulness of the perspective he represents, the soldier is never labeled "the enemy," never found to be intrinsically worthy of hate. The hatefulness lies in his relation to the landscape and its implication for, and of, the speaker (whose use of the French language serves sufficiently to identify her). In the clear-eyed restraint that characterizes her use of illustrations, scrupulously respecting distinctions that serve, Weil's attitude calls to mind that of Camus, writing his *Lettres à un ami allemand* (1943–1944), that is, letters addressed to a German still as a friend, though expressing opposition to Nazism, and whose intellectual integrity, as Isabelle de Courtivron observes, cost him dearly, as Weil's did her: "His story reminds us that some men and women were destroyed precisely because they could not force themselves into taking unequivocal ideological stances, and could not judge human situations in Manichean terms" (14). A sense of moral responsibility does not simplify the world or make judgment easier; distinctions must still be made.

If the self is aware of intersecting with the world—establishing its connection with a given landscape, a written symbol, a piece of metal—it cannot entertain any kind of projection in its dealings with others:

> To love one's neighbor as oneself does not mean to love all beings equally, because I don't love equally all the modes of my own existence. Nor to never cause them to suffer, because I don't refuse causing myself to suffer. But to have with each the relation of one way of conceiving the universe with another

way of conceiving the universe, and not to a part of the universe. A man ten steps away from me is something separated from me by a distance (ten steps), but also another perspective from which all things appear. The relation between me and another man can never be analogous to the blind man and his stick, nor to the inverse relationship; it is in this way that slavery is contrary to nature and to reason.

War is a way of imposing another reading of sensations, an act on the imagination of another. (OC 6:1:295)

Weil's thinking does not stray from her mathematical model, allowing her to infer the multifaceted self's resemblance to the world it observes, and to apply religious precept in a way that brushes aside considerations of persons or social order—the levels she will label "inferior" in "La Personne et le sacré"—to focus on the individual consciousness in its integrity. The possibilities of overlap and permeability are not envisioned; the wholeness of the other's unique perspective, distinct from one's own, must be acknowledged. Agreement on certain issues does not mean identity. Weil thus posits our essential solitude; if points of intersection with others do exist, it is at the margins of the self, along the partition—like writing, that travels to the edges of the space between beings. She substitutes a vocabulary of abstraction for one of affect, speaking of time and space, not of desire and intimacy. Altruism does not stem from mere benevolence or religious devotion. Idealism and sentimentality banished, identity of viewpoints precluded, love of neighbor emerges as a principle congruent with one's sense of the world and with intellectual integrity. The necessary primacy of the subjectivity—for it is all each of us have, as our starting point, for exploring the world—makes the barbarity of slavery apparent, and from there Weil easily returns to the perception that launches these notebooks.

The impersonality of her interpretation of the injunction to love one's neighbor provides a way of dealing with the German soldier's presence on the social level without being false. One need not feel warmly about him, nor refrain from working toward his defeat. But it is reductive to focus solely on his nationalist ideology, however repellent it may be; it represents only part of his view of the universe, even if he himself may have narrowed its full scope. Adding the soldier to the landscape, as reality obliges, does nothing to reduce the complexity of the equation; the sum is a painful loss of human freedom all around.

In examining the stance Weil maps out in the Marseilles notebooks, one observes the use of a mathematical vocabulary and rigor that serves to uphold, ultimately, as a principle of justice, the speaker's position. The positive use of time and space coexists with the consciousness' painful awakening: "Space and time are in a sense only thoughts, and at the same time that which shackles the thinking being without possible liberation" (*OC* 6:1:294). The individual perspective each one holds is still proof of one's reality, the incontrovertible fact. This is not the argument Weil makes, already moved to another register, in "La Personne et le sacré," where she refers instead to the inviolate particle of the self that retains its innocence, and where she draws, though not exclusively, on vocabulary and imagery more commonly associated with Christian religious texts. Here, in the notebooks, her fiercely independent thought, matched in its intensity and resourcefulness by her astonishing gifts as a writer, gives rise to a dazzling display of mastery and in no way predicates her departure. If the direction Weil's thought later forcefully took was not inevitable, as this point of departure suggests, the evidence of a progression confirms the open-endedness of her inquiry and at the same time preserves an alternate viewpoint itself of inestimable worth. The same dispassionateness with which she gazes upon human perspective, not yet seen in an unrelievedly negative light, allows for the making of painful discriminations that probably refer obliquely to her work with foreign refugees in Marseilles:

> When one renders service to beings uprooted in this way [by extreme suffering] and receives ill treatment, ingratitude, betrayal in return, one is simply being subjected to a small part of their misery ["malheur"]. . . . When that happens, one must tolerate it as one tolerates misery, without connecting it to specific persons, because it isn't to be connected to them. There is something impersonal in quasi-infernal misery as there is in perfection. (*OC* 6:2:356)

Recognizing that these people "have lost the clothing of character" (*OC* 6:2:356), Weil attributes to them their humanity, just as she does not let the Nazi uniform act as a shield to ward off her gaze; appearances are but one side of the cube.

Close in spirit is Char's meditation:

> One should not love men in order to be of real assistance to them. Only want to make this expression in their gaze better when it rests upon others more impoverished than they, to prolong by a second that agreeable minute of their life. From this step onward, and with each root treated, their respiration would become more serene. Especially not wholly keep them from those painful paths, the effort of [climbing] which is succeeded by evidence of the truth through tears and fruits. (207)

While Weil would leave aside as of secondary importance those notations related to quantity or modulation—the extra second of happiness, the more peaceful breathing—she shares with Char, who distributed arms throughout his region and enjoyed the protection of sympathetic villagers, the same sense of the limitation of one's effectiveness, of the reality of poverty, of the need to cultivate both the compassionate gaze and the spiritual roots of the other's being, and the same acknowledgment of pain as an unavoidable form of access to truth. Char's evocation of "tears and fruits," like Weil's of suffering and joy, reminds us that thought at one extreme must reach to encompass the other if it is to speak to the human condition at large, a goal they also share. Char knows too that "poetry is not sovereign everywhere" (207), an admission having much in common with Weil's exhortation to "[s]trip oneself of the imaginary royalty of the world, in order to reduce oneself to the point one occupies in space and time" (*OC* 6:2:308). Such a concordance of views between poet and philosopher, though not explained by the image of the cube, suggests the aptness of Weil's inclusion of art in her frame of reference as she develops her notion of reading, which posits as indispensable the existence of a right reading.

As Florence de Lussy writes, "To read the *Cahiers* of Simone Weil straight through is, in effect, to participate, not without exaltation, in a powerful forward march of thought" (*OC* 6:1:13); the assurance of the writing, the vastness of scope and erudition, the fearless display of intuition, the rapidity of discovery and assimilation—all astound, disarm, excite. Burned into every page is the conviction that intellectual freedom is preserved only in the exercise of it, for "[l]iberty as such is not an object of daydream" (*OC* 6:2:206). Underlying this explosion of creativity is also a sense of the fragility of the enterprise; not only can a gray-green uniform mutilate a landscape, but a self has no permanence: "Nothing more intolerable to man than the awareness of his own modifiability" (*OC* 6:2:250). The speaker's authority rests in part on a sharp sense of contingency, of the fortuitousness of the inquiry; Weil goes right to the essential. The impersonality of the language at once deflects attention from superfluous consideration of the author's person ("Madame . . . *who* are you?," as a reader was moved to ask) and gives the impression that she is already speaking from beyond the grave. In fact, she was all too aware of speaking from a specific point in time and space, one subject, at any moment, to erasure: "It is impossible to be proud . . . of one's intellect at the moment one truly exercises it. . . . For one knows that, should one become an idiot the next instant and for the rest of one's life, the truth continues to exist" (*OC* 6:2:491). However precious intellectual gifts might be, we do not possess them truly; and Weil will be moved to look elsewhere for greater treasure, as she was to write to Gilbert Kahn: "Why should I attach much importance to that part of my intelligence that anyone, absolutely anyone, by means of whips and chains, or walls and locks, or a piece of paper covered with certain characters, can take away from me? . . . If there is some other thing that proves irreducible, it is that which is infinitely precious" (*VSW* 568).

All of existence is precarious:

> Attachment is nothing other than insufficiency in the sense of reality. One is attached to the possession of a thing because one believes that if one ceases to possess it, it ceases to exist. Thus that woman who, passing before a line of people waiting, stopped there because, if she had passed by, the fish being distributed would have been lost. She thought that the food she and her family did not eat did not exist. Many people do not feel with all their soul that there is an utter difference between the annihilation of a city and their irremediable exile from that city. (*OC* 6:2:491)

All the givens of our existence are precisely that—givens—and so they can be taken away. But we take it for granted that they are

ours, have their being in our possession. Our willed ignorance of
the possibility of a complete reversal of fortune is at once comical
and poignant, for the magic we wishfully work in our minds has no
effect on reality. If the woman approaches the fishmonger's as though
to obtain fish dependent on her for their existence, so the exile
(from Paris?) mistakes a devastating personal loss for a limitless
one, for the city, with all its architecture and history, has not been
expunged. Were the city destroyed, so also would be its irretriev-
able collective soul. Our mental landscapes require constant revis-
iting. People and things exist independently of us. One of the goals
Weil sets for herself and for undaunted readers of her notebooks is
to root out the notion of a fixed, reliable order of things corresponding to our convenience: "If with a gesture I knock over a pile of
books, it will require me time and effort to put them back; the
possibility of my being condemned to twenty years in prison is a
form of the same necessity, which stems from the nature of time"
(OC 6:1:241). One's location, one's intellect, one's next meal are all
subject to time and chance. Weil does not set herself above the
woman anxious to feed her family, the exiles longing for home.

If the notebooks are, on one level, an astonishing outpouring of
thought dazzling to behold, to the beholder they are also that
brusque gesture overturning received ideas, false expectations, the
mild and not so mild subterfuges crafted by the intellect; they expose the mind's poverty and condemn its compromises. What, in
the midst of desolation, constitutes integrity, intellectual integrity
and moral integrity together, these works seem to be asking; what
does it mean to hold the German soldier and the French landscape
together in the mind? Or to be fully cognizant of that distance of
ten steps between one's own position and another's in relation to
the world? How can one justly consider other persons, when one
kind of clothing has been put on, when another kind has been lost?
What is the relation of knowledge, of work, of sensations to a right
reading of one's location in time and space? What forces are set in
motion when one takes up the pen, the sword, the challenge to love
one's neighbor? How can the mind extricate itself from the web of
the imagination, even as it suffers the wounds of defeat? What is to
be gleaned from history and sacred texts, mathematics and physics,
art and literature, that is authentic sustenance? What is most precious about the intellect, and what price for its use and for its free-

dom must one be willing to pay? Is wholeness to be found? What is inscribed on the coin of suffering exacted in tribute by a deterministic universe, the only face we see of a remote, unbending God?

As these questions and others urgently arose in the blackness of the France of Vichy, Weil strove to reconcile her sense of reality with her religious aspirations and her intellectual vocation:

A man whose whole family perished by torture, who was himself tortured for a long time in a concentration camp. Or a sixteenth-century Indian who alone escaped from the extermination of his entire people. Such men, if they once believed in divine mercy, either no longer believe in it or conceive of it in a wholly different way. I haven't gone through such things. But I do know they exist; given that fact, what difference [is there]? It comes down, or must or ought to come down, to the same thing. (C 3:49)

Confronting the brutal evidence, Weil posits as equivalent experience in the present and experience in the past, experience of an event and knowledge of it as fact. The survivor of the camp is close by, the Indian known only through historical documents, those requiring the reader "to read between the lines, to transport oneself fully, with complete self-forgetfulness, into the events evoked there, to stop and examine at length the small, revealing things and discern their full significance" (E 283–84). The interpretation of texts— the work of the intellect—brings us into contact with reality in a way as significant as the evidence of our senses, with as much validity as the testimony of the present. Reading the signs around us, reading documents of the past—these alter our landscape, these are lessons in our own "modifiability." Still, with our imperfect materials—ourselves—we cannot fully know the other. Continuing her reflection, Weil asks of thought a guiding star, a counterweight:

I must wish to have, to be inclined to have, of divine mercy a conception that does not fade and does not change, whatever the event destiny sends upon me and around me, one that can be communicated to any human being (in granting myself the ability, which I don't have, to communicate something) without being to him an outrage.

Inspiration alone can give such a conception, but it is for oneself to renounce all those that are not that [inspired] one. (C 3:49)

Of her philosophy she requires both absoluteness and expressibility, something immutable and yet accessible to all and consonant with each one's sense of reality. Her work would be the juncture of transcendence and language, rooted firmly in the world, Platonic in reach. The proposal for front-line nurses, with its veiled meaning, begins to shed even this lofty ideal, a movement prefigured, perhaps, in the self-doubting, self-disparaging aside. All the same, even as her concept of perspective moves beyond comparison with the cube, beyond the multiplicity of single viewpoints fixed in time and space, Weil affirms the work of the intellect, its powers of discernment, its extension through the pen. With the poets and writers of her generation who resisted the extinction of their thought, she had begun to create, as Arendt has said, that "public space . . . where freedom could appear." It remains a space with room for reader and writer alike. In Char's memorable words: "At every meal taken together, we invite freedom to sit down. The seat remains empty, but the place stays set" (206). In the notebooks, this "mass of fragments," a product of their era as much as anything she ever wrote, Weil renounces the closed narrative for the open book. As Paul Celan, another contemporary, says simply: "I cannot see any basic difference between a handshake and a poem" (26). Her poetry and her writings on poetics, many also appearing in the notebooks, confirm this affinity with that most elemental art.

5

Poetry and Poetics

In a recent essay, poet Louise Glück alludes to the error of investing poetic energies "in conclusion, in axiom, in heroic grandeur. Poetic intelligence lacks . . . such focused investment in conclusion, being naturally wary of its own assumptions. It derives its energy from a willingness to discard conclusion in the face of evidence, its willingness, in fact, to discard anything" (95). What appears as pure recklessness is, from such a perspective, simple honesty: the refusal to affirm anything for the sake of form, or to please an audience, or to give false consolation, especially to oneself. It means resisting the pull of rhythm and facile sonorities when these lead to groundless assertion. The poet proceeds, in Dickinson's words, "from Plank to Plank," from word to word, line to line, poem to poem, or paragraph to paragraph, all safety at risk in the venture. Weil early on recognized, from her analytical standpoint, this essential precariousness of artistic and intellectual inquiry, and indeed of individual progress as experienced in the succession of discrete moments—a subject inviting literary treatment, as she instinctively knew—when writing in her factory journal:

What counts in a human life is not the events governing the course of years, or even months, or even days. It's the way in which each minute is linked to the next and what it costs each person in his or her body, heart, and soul—and above all in the exercise of the faculty of attention—to bring this linking about minute by minute.

If I were to write a novel, I'd be doing something entirely new. (*OC* 2:2:267)

The exposed journey into the unknown, beyond appearances, deprived of security, is related in kind to the one undertaken by Weil as she opens her Marseilles notebooks, gazing bravely and dispassionately upon a German soldier. Discovering one's world fundamentally changed, newly inhospitable, requires the jettisoning of old maps, the acknowledgment that boundaries are susceptible to being redrawn. Clearsightedness in the assessment—that is to say, integrity—demands a corresponding suspension of allegiances; "Poetry is not for sale" (*E* 294), Weil will write in London.

Following the movement of the mind as it receives sensations and makes moral choices, Weil's notebooks record the drama of a journey toward self-knowledge, an ordeal to be suffered—that is, both gone through and painfully earned—and freshly committed to writing. Abrupt and shattering insights, bold illustrations leap from the pages with all the freshness of discovery; and, had she indeed taken up the writing of a novel conceived with the same openendedness, its originality might well have been striking. But disappointingly, when venturing upon what formally is literary terrain, Weil seems to take refuge in convention. The pedagogical element is frequently allowed to prevail; the parabolic "Prologue" sketches out characters too brittle to bear the weight of reference to transcendent experience; notes related to *Venise sauvée* indicate the extent to which carefully articulated intentions, more than internal dramatic considerations, govern the writing of the play; her poetry, in its conception closely tied to traditional forms, expounds elements of her philosophy earnestly and transparently, without the breathtaking animation and subtlety characteristic of her finest prose. Commitment to conclusiveness, manifest in form and content, freezes the flow of thought—and its play as well. The psychological element per se holds no interest for her—it exists only to be decreated—

and the imagination, source of illusion, is to be banished. Weil's poetic gifts as a writer, wonderfully at home elsewhere in her prose, where intellectual freedom reigns supreme, seem to desert her, or at least to abruptly cede place to her philosophical convictions, in the presence of nominally poetic forms.

Philosophy and poetry are by no means strangers, although the impulse toward expression arising within them may well spring from different sources: "If the philosopher's world is this present world plus thought, then the poet's world is this present world plus imagination" (864), writes Wallace Stevens. But philosophical discourse may possess poetry in its own right. The austere beauty of Weil's prose is not, for instance, a function of restraint of the imaginative faculty as befitting the work of a philosopher; rather, it stems at least in part from a helplessness before scraps of evidence, a poverty of means imaginatively overcome by the oblique perspective detecting unanticipated logic. The superimposition of soldier upon landscape, studied microscopically, serves to illustrate the workings of a law of perception; the silence of the vagrant before the urbane judge ("La Personne et le sacré") opens to inspection the abyss that is a hollow system of criminal justice. The same attentiveness to the influence of unseen processes or motivations masked by incongruities leads to brilliant intuitions, astonishing linkages that reward the reader of the essays and notebooks—and to an impasse in what would be poetic discourse, freighted with explanation, constricted in point of view, discovery—preordained—reduced to a point of reference.

Even though poetry was not Weil's true calling, a verdict contrary to her own assessment (poet Jean Tortel, who knew her in Marseilles, attests: "I truly think she would have sacrificed her whole work for the few poems she wrote" [*VSW* 531]), beauty plays the indispensable mediating role in her metaphysics. In a note written in New York, she asserts that artistic creation is not merely a function of human consciousness; it signifies entry into the moral dimension: "There is a thing the devil cannot do, I think. Inspire a painter to make a painting that, placed in the cell of a man condemned to solitary confinement, would still be a comfort to him after twenty years" (*CS* 313). The spiritual nourishment given by the painting, and continually renewed by it, confirms the genius of its inspiration; Weil's is an aesthetics of invisible weights and balances, these forces implicit in the imprint of a mind upon matter. In her hastily sketched illustration, artist and prisoner do not directly communicate; a social context for reception of the work is lacking, as is any consideration of the artist's *œuvre* as such. These things, like questions of technique, do not bear discussing (cf. Celan's comment: "[C]raft, like cleanliness in general, is the condition of all poetry" [25]); the essential act of contemplation, the viewer's privilege, is private. As in other of Weil's texts, immobility is designated as a precondition for enlightenment; like the narrator of "Prologue," the prisoner is confined to his room; like the voiceless dog silently barking to save his unconscious master ("La Personne et le sacré"), the painting beckons from the wall. The extremity of solitude and deprivation strips the mind of its defenses and exposes it to the workings of inspiration. This rare allowance for true consolation has much in common with a nonhypothetical instance from Char's *Feuillets d'Hypnos*:

> The color reproduction of Georges de La Tour's *The Prisoner* that I pinned on the chalk wall of the room where I work seems, as time goes by, to reflect its meaning in our condition. It tugs at the heart, but how replenishing! For the past two years, not a single *réfractaire* [French citizen refusing to report for "obligatory labor" in Nazi Germany] who, going by the door, hasn't had his eyes burned by the proofs of that candle. The woman explains, the imprisoned man listens. The words falling from that red angel's earthly silhouette are essential words, words that immediately bring succor. . . . Thanks to Georges de La Tour who mastered the shadows of Hitler with a dialogue between human beings. (218)

Char's attention to detail also pins down something else: the political context his story shares with Weil's more theoretical musing, further indication that Weil's thoughts remained fully entrenched in occupied Europe. The very real danger of imprisonment always a step away (a step the man in Weil's example is no longer at liberty to take), the relevance of art to the situation of those taking costly moral positions, the sustenance it gives, its increasing importance with the passing of time (even the reproduction communicates forcefully)—these reflections of the urgency of the moment, as appre-

hended by minds alert equally to the aesthetic and ethical dimensions, may be seen to confirm the existence of a common ground for
poet and philosopher—Stevens's "this present world." Just as Weil's
evocation of solitude is typical of her, so Char's celebration of dialogue, as found within the painting and in his comradely salute to
the artist, is consonant with his sense of the essentially communal
nature of effective resistance (as seen in his remark, "I fiercely loved
my fellow human beings that day" [206]—a statement unimaginable
in Weil's later works, except, perhaps, in connection with her glow-
ing praise of Londoners). This contrast of temperaments does not
obscure a fundamental agreement on the aesthetic plane; in the excerpts, both paintings provide loyal companionship and light, and to
the receptive eye, they openly reveal their spiritual dimension.

   In the eyes of these contemporaries, this association of art with
divine agency—removed from the demonic element, accommodating the visiting angel—lifts it above the individual predicament. To
that predicament art holds out the possibility of explanation; like de
La Tour's prisoner, one need only listen. Keeping vigil in the viewer's
behalf, radiating its constant presence in the midst of clear-cut
oppositions on the moral plane (shadows/light, devil/divine inspiration, Hitler/the imprisoned, *réfractaires*), the work of art gives
strength to those allied with the good by transcending the limitations of the present moment. It will freely retain meaning over time,
pierce through the walls surrounding the soul, become for it a
window. In keeping with the poet and the philosopher's determination to overcome their country's defeat, it posits a world beyond
the immediate one: the reality of justice, even when evidence is
absent. Because works can be suffused with redeeming meaning,
the treasurableness of art is certain.

   In the case of Weil's philosophy, this affirmation constitutes a
rare positive note, but it is not an expansive one. This is manifest
not only in her rejection of surrealism and her disinterest in the
representation of psychological states, as in Proust, but also in her
lack of allowance for other aesthetic possibilities. Weil's entire preoccupation is with art's contact with the infinite; in the absence of
this point of intersection or the aspiration toward it, she has no
sympathy for the artist. To be reminded of the exclusiveness of this
approach, one need only think of Elizabeth Bishop's elderly and
abandoned Crusoe, whose "knife there on the shelf—/it reeked of

meaning, like a crucifix./ . . . /Now it won't look at me at all./The living soul has dribbled away" (166). Is it our dullness or the inevitably finite nature of the meaning we invest in objects that makes us turn from them in the end, the poem seems to ask; Crusoe's solitude is a measure of life itself, not of a distance from a world beyond the heavens. The twenty years of contemplation Weil affords her hypothetical prisoner locates meaning in the painting itself; but in the twenty-first year should he cease to draw comfort from it, this failure would point to a defect of eye or inspiration, an improper relation to the divine, not to the inevitable result of living or even to the possibility of a changed perspective. The dynamics of artistic creation and communication remain constant. Weil's aesthetics is resolutely Platonic and Christian in its orientation, her response to historical emergency at once the impulse to transcend (mysticism) and the effort to salvage (a measure sometimes mistaken for reactionary conservatism, as she ruefully acknowledges ["Lettre aux *Cahiers du Sud*" 354]). In terms of poetics, hers is not an attempt to stake out new ground or to question biases inherent in values and vocabularies she desperately wishes to preserve.

Weil has not demystified art; she has sanctified it: "Utmost attentiveness is what constitutes the creative faculty in man, and utmost attentiveness is none other than religious" (C 3:59). Bishop's work alone, however, indicates that artistic awareness may proceed quite scrupulously without necessarily finding religious meaning in what it examines. Weil subsumes art into her larger categories of belief. If exile in this world (*ici-bas*) is for her the incontrovertible truth of human experience, it is a relation to a supervening reality, by nature something fixed, mathematical. The immobility of the work of art and the fixity of the contemplative gaze correspond, in her aesthetics, to our unchanging state in this pitiless universe. Artistic scrutiny of this world, because it will at least implicitly acknowledge this condition, can re-create the link between the harshness of truth and the perception of beauty: "Art. Poetry. To make horrible things lovable as horrible things, simply because they exist, is to learn the love of God. *Iliad*." (C 3:69). Weil's poem "Nécessité" ("Necessity"), written in Marseilles and incorporated into her notebooks (*OC* 6:2:147–48), clearly means to illustrate this principle:

NECESSITY

The cycle of days in the deserted sky turning
In silence watched by mortal eyes
Gaping mouth here below, where each hour is burning
So many cruel and beseeching cries;

All the stars slow in the steps of their dance,
The only fixed dance, mute brilliance on high,
In spite of us formless, nameless, without cadence,
Too perfect, no fault to belie;

Toward them, suspended, our anger is vain.
Quench our thirst, if you must break our hearts.
Clamoring and desiring, their circle draws us in their train;
Our brilliant masters were forever victors.

Tear flesh apart, chains of pure clarity.
Nailed without a cry to the fixed point of the North,
Naked soul exposed to all injury,
May we obey you unto death.

Reminiscent of Weil's claim to being "a badly cut-off piece of God" (*VSW* 682), this poem in the original presents an image of the human condition in lines of eleven syllables, one short of the twelve characteristic of the alexandrine of French poetry and classical drama—an odd, disjointed meter that persistently calls attention to its imperfection. It is as if the poet deliberately maims her creation in order to ensure its truthfulness; in a poem devoted to the realm of necessity, where determinism rules unchecked, it would be false to project a sense of fullness or the possibility of transcendence, even on the level of form. These signs of hopefulness have been taken away; each line haunted by its absent, unpronounceable syllable cries out the reality of subjection and disfigurement. Although the effect is not one of mysteriousness, Weil is sensitive to poetry's demands; in Dickinson's words, "Nature is a Haunted House—but Art—a House that tries to be haunted" (2:554)—but neither domicile can long contain a mystic. The poem's one perfect figure—the circle of passing days (the "cycle" so called in a variant [*P* 33]), perceived by us in the stars' immutable dance—does not include us. By way of contrast, Weil does compose in alexandrines in "Les Astres" ("Stars") (*OC* 6:2:285, 405), in which "their divine light" is internalized by the speakers (Weil's typical "we") in the last line of the poem. This formally balanced work continues and completes the reflection of "Nécessité" in that Stoic acceptance is followed by all-encompassing enlightenment, recapitulating the poet's mystical trajectory. But first, in the absence of inner illumination, there is only darkness and suffering, the halting gait of fettered slaves; this is the image, aural and thematic, of "Nécessité." If Valéry admired in Weil's early poetry the evidence of a "will to compose" (*P* 10), this work demonstrates its persistence.

Portraying the futility of our abandonment on earth, Weil's poem posits a separate heavenly sphere unmoved by endless human cries. When, broken in mind and body, we take in its indifferent silence, the will to obedience has been achieved. The dance of the stars induces stasis; "too perfect," they are disorienting; how can they guide us in a world that is fallen, utterly foreign to them? Immune to human science ("in spite of us formless"), they defeat our small powers of logic and observation. The poet writes on a blank slate that, like the work of the astronomers, will be wiped clean. The cycle of stars implicates our extinction; they have always won. The first and last nouns of the poem—"cycle" and "death"—distill the essence of a bitter acknowledgment. Words of Celan again come to mind: "Poetry, ladies and gentlemen: what an eternalization of nothing but mortality, and in vain" (52).

In keeping with her injunction that "writers need not be professors of morals, but they must express the human condition" ("Lettre aux *Cahiers du Sud*" 356), Weil undertakes her appointed task along the broadest possible lines, elucidating principles as opposed to particulars—an approach evident in the illustration involving a painting, so very different, in terms of descriptiveness, from Char's. Indeed, the poem is set up as a kind of problem requiring a solution, albeit one precluding human happiness. In a musically striking line, the invocation of "chains of pure clarity" ("chaînes de clarté pure") does not invite us to picture the aurora borealis but rather to link the reality of human subjection with the starry sky, two aspects of the same necessity. The imagination is not permitted to stray.

As in the case of the "Prologue," it again proves instructive to compare Weil's work with that of Baudelaire, the opening stanza of

"Nécessité" immediately calling to mind, for a variety of reasons, the famous poems "Correspondances" ("Correspondences") and "L'Albatros" ("The Albatross"). Behind all of these poems looms the specter of the Romantic will to ascribe to nature the trace, if not the memory, of human experience—a will necessarily doomed, as expressed in the anguish of the speaker in Lamartine's "Le Lac" ("The Lake"), oppressed by the intolerable prospect of a past love's absorption into unremembering time. Weil's universe crushes the spirit of rebellion, revealing an implacable mechanism; in Baudelaire, while the speaker is never unaffected by his surroundings and revels in sensuality, he is some way supremely and audaciously detached. To subsume nature into the realm of human consciousness, to make of it a source of stimuli conducive to our entertainment, is to subvert the apparent order. The narrator of *Le Spleen de Paris*, leaning out his garret window, is no stranger to vertigo.

Gustave Thibon remarks of Weil: "Her self [*moi*] was like a word she had perhaps managed to *erase* but that still remained *underlined*" (*VSW* 570). In "Nécessité," the "mortal eyes" (*regards des mortels*) of the first stanza, still plural and not yet simplified into the singular "death" (*mort*) of the final line, give anonymous proof of our existence; but each gaze is a critical one, implicitly judging the unresponsive heavens. If an individual speaker is lacking, glaringly present is the unforgiving stance, the cries of pain its many echos; the shackles are in place. Necessity erases each of us, and we burn in silent anger, the only way for us to imitate the stars. Weil has brought the object of contemplation—the cold, inaccessible stars—into a process of internal combustion, one identical with self-negation. The point of ignition is not specified, and eventual extinction is a condition of seeing, our eyes by definition "mortal." Alive, we have no vitality; our energy is almost spent.

Whereas Weil's poem drives home its inescapable conclusion, relentless after the manner of a fate consigning us to exile and death, Baudelaire's "Correspondances" (1:11) evokes a permeable architecture through which the speaker and his species freely wander:

> Nature is a temple where living pillars
> Sometimes release confused phrases;
> Man passes there through forests of symbols
> Observing him with familiar gazes.

Baudelaire, who in "Recueillement" ("Recollection") proclaims that "the vile multitude of mortals/Under the whip of Pleasure . . . / Goes to gather remorse in servile celebration" (1:141), is hardly uninfected by the pessimism characteristic also of Weil's general outlook. But he is not so quick to strip the world, and his poetry, of human resonance; observation and indistinct speech are reflected back to us; we are allowed the ecstasy of multiple evocations, the luxury of discriminating among various sensations and our memories of them. It is making a virtue—or artificial paradise—out of necessity. As in the prose pieces previously examined, the aesthetic and ethical senses come into proximity, but Baudelaire knowingly succumbs to the charm of the former; Weil, attempting synthesis in "Prologue" and in her poetry, cannot compromise the demands of the latter. Baudelaire opens up a constricted universe of the senses; Weil explicates a closed, constricting one. In "Correspondances," Baudelaire chooses, among many others, impressions having "the expansion of infinite things," reducing the infinite to manageable, delectable proportions (he goes on to cite "amber, musk, benzoin, and incense"); in "Nécessité," Weil's logic leads implacably to exposed immobility, torn flesh daring the universe to make of it an untouchable thing. If the speaker in "Correspondances" can nonchalantly recall the "flesh of children" as one association among many, Weil's battered humanity seems magnetically attracted to the site of its own reduction. "Zero is our maximum," she says elsewhere.

Baudelaire's "L'Albatros" (1:9–10), akin to Weil's "Nécessité" in its stark depiction of humiliation and tyranny, allows the promptings of symbol to emerge where Weil rigorously clamps them down. The deliberate, sordid cruelty of the sailors comes naturally to them—"Often, for amusement," begins the poem; taunting the trapped bird, "one irritates his beak with a pipe,/the other mimics, limping, the cripple who once flew." Unjustly ship-bound, hampered by the weight of his wings, the albatross resembles the poet: "Exiled on land amidst jeers,/His giant's wings prevent him from walking." The inharmonious, vernacular *"brûle-gueule"* (literally, mouth-scorcher; pipe) grates on the ear, as does Weil's characterization of the world as a *"[g]ueule ouverte"* (gaping mouth), both images representing an assault on voice and appetite. The tortured albatross-poet cannot sing; the heaving cries of the furnace of oppression are formless and unquenchable. But the poet's plight is made vivid and unforgettable; Weil's vision of injustice recedes into generalized statement. The bitterness of these striking lines of "Nécessité"— "Our brilliant masters were forever victors./Tear flesh apart, chains of pure clarity"—is diluted by the ensuing language, neutral in tonality if conclusive in terms of logic. If impersonality on one level signifies a rejection of the decadence of which unrestricted association is a symptom ("Correspondances"), it also appears to reflect a certain paralysis of the imagination. Distrust of the source of poetry, consistent with her loyalty to Plato, perhaps made it necessary for Weil to always work hard, intellectually, at her poetry, will it into existence, rather than listen for it, hard work of a different kind. Felicity seems to be denied.

But if Weil's poetry shows the withering effects of a harsh mental ascesis, there is much in the rich harvest of her prose that has given comfort—and pause—to poets and writers, compelling them to take renewed measure of their art. Seamus Heaney writes in *The Redress of Poetry*:

> [H]er whole book [*Gravity and Grace*] is informed by the idea of counterweighting, of balancing out the forces, of redress—tilting the scales of reality towards some transcendent equilibrium. And in the activity of poetry too, there is a tendency to place a counter-reality in the scales—a reality which may be only imagined but which nevertheless has a weight because it is imagined within the gravitational pull of the actual and can therefore hold its own and balance out against the historical situation. This redressing effect of poetry comes from its being a glimpsed alternative, a revelation of potential that is denied or constantly threatened by circumstances. And sometimes, of course, it happens that such a revelation, once enshrined in the poem, remains as a standard for the poet, so that he or she must then submit to the strain of bearing witness in his or her own life to the plane of consciousness established in the poem. (3–4)

Heaney goes on in his essay to cite the example of George Herbert by way of illustration, an unerring choice in this context. What Weil offers poets as they practice their art, as distinct from her dogmatic strictures on the nature of greatness, and if Heaney's remarks may be taken as representative, is the assurance of the reality of the world of mind and spirit in which poetry participates, a reality whose laws can be studied and formulated. Indeed, Weil remarks upon the writings of the mystics as being precisely the documentation of such laws. Inspired by Weil's unalterable faith in the existence of that one atom of goodness residing in each human soul, Heaney transfers the source of his trust to the same soul's product, poetry; that which is "only imagined" is as real and irreducible as a grain of sand, and it truly contains the potential for redress. There is something quantitative, just, and reassuring in this image of corrected balance; the measured words of poets have measurable effect on history and individual character. Poetry is thus a force, an "activity," one that may play a part in bringing about the good. Like Weil's, Heaney's view gives primacy to harmony, order, the concordance of art and justice, the rigorous requirements of integrity—all of which, expressed with a lofty seriousness, point to its European character.

Would Weil herself accept Heaney's transposition? Surely she, who presumes Mallarmé's sainthood (*E* 297), would approve of his acknowledgment of the demands of personal integrity placed upon the individual poet whose work accedes to a higher "plane of consciousness." The identity of artistic and moral genius she herself posits in *L'Enracinement* (295–96). But it seems doubtful that, toward the end of her life, she would have so readily attributed to the "only imagined," however responsibly derived, the same potential for redress as the divinely created particle of the good; and it is here perhaps that poets must necessarily misread her (if they do indeed misread her). For Weil, the inspired work of art only reflects, if reflect it does, the working of the good at large: "But fortunately for us, there is a reflective property in matter" (*CO* 362). The world's injustice is too great a thing to place upon the small scales of poetry; a poem—like a painting—is, however, a thing small enough to place in our prison cells of mind or concrete, giving us strength to cultivate the faculty of attention: "Most certainly a page covered with pencil marks is not a thing more beautiful than the universe, but it is a thing made to our measure" (*C* 3:162). To achieve such a thing as tipping "the scales of reality," we must leave our literature behind: "How else would we be able to hear God's silence if the noise here below meant something?" (*C* 3:274).

The Weil who so tirelessly promoted her proposal for front-line nurses was prepared to leave everything behind, leap out of life and language in response to a mystical intuition far more radical than any poetic one. In one of her last letters, written just after she had broken off ties with the Free French, she explains:

> Intellects wholly, exclusively given over and devoted to the truth are not able to be put to use by any human being, including the one in whom they reside. I don't have the possibility of using my own intelligence; how could I put it at the disposal of [André] Philip [her former supervisor]? It is using me instead, and it obeys without reservation—at least I hope that this is the case— that which appears to it to be the light of truth. It obeys day by day, instant by instant, and my will never exercises any action over it. (*VSW* 684–85)

"[D]ay by day, instant by instant"—this is the language of the twenty-six-year-old working in the Renault factory, defining "[w]hat counts in a human life," prepared to observe that life in its most subtle and inconspicuous manifestation, those moments ordinarily escaping detection. Fineness of perception, a great gift, is not in itself an orientation. It was intellectual integrity, as she lived out its requirements moment by moment, that for Weil formed the connective tissue of her conscious life, exacting a terrible cost in "body, heart, and soul." In the domain of poetic creation, where other forces have their part to play, its exclusiveness took its toll and, among the evidence, Weil's vaguely intuited novel never did come into being. But most remarkably in her notebooks, she fulfills that early promise and brings to fruition that extraordinary attentiveness to the mind's subtleties, illuminating, along with so many other things, psychological processes involved in the act of writing that have rarely been so fully and scrupulously described. From this vantage point, with its closeness to the ground, Weil's writing takes on a forcefulness and a poetic éclat that establish her authority as a reader of the inner life, a stature already apparent in those first pages written in Marseilles where we find her taking stock, calmly and intently, of a moral and political disaster. Weil's insights into this sphere where ethics and aesthetics come into play bear comparison on equal terms with those of the poet Marina Tsvetaeva (1892–1941), her great Russian contemporary.

In her magnificent essay "Art in the Light of Conscience" (1932), Tsvetaeva begins by paying tribute to conventional wisdom: "What is certain: a work of art is a work of nature, just as much born and not made. . . . Female gestation and the artist's gestation of his work have been talked of so often they don't need insisting on: all know— and all know correctly" (149). Weil would agree: "One writes as one gives birth; one can't help making the supreme effort" (OC 6:2:129). Something new comes into being; the writer is the necessary medium.

Tsvetaeva acknowledges the artist's full responsibility for "the work of his hands" and observes that commonly such work "is supposed to be illumined by the light of reason and conscience" (150). That is the general assumption, but she herself stops short of making any commitment in that direction. Do aesthetics and ethics fully converge in artistic creation? Must the work of art proceed under the same rule of moral law as does the person who would avoid evil? For Weil, these troubling distinctions have already been dissolved: "Now, nothing is so essential to human life, for all people and at all instants, as good and evil. When literature takes a stance by which it becomes indifferent to the opposition of good and evil, it betrays its purpose and can lay no claim to excellence" ("Lettre aux Cahiers du Sud" 356–57). Literature does not merely exist, it has a purpose: already we move beyond the simple fact of the artist contemplating in its newness the fruit of his or her labor. Already Weil's thought has flown to a lofty perch, looking down on human shortcoming as measured by immutable laws—in this case, the requirement of writers to "express the human condition" ("Lettre aux Cahiers du Sud" 356). Her words are also an expression of disgust prompted by the falseness of a literature unable to squarely face the reality of the French defeat and its consequences. From this compromised ground, which cannot otherwise be surmounted, she moves vertically.

As a philosopher, Weil is not bound by the same considerations as the artist, who inhabits a smaller world of particulars. Even in the area of illustrations, Weil roughly sketches her prison cell; Char lovingly reconstructs his. At the same time, as a writer giving shape to her work, she is free to enter into this more specialized world by means of introspection. This we often see in her notebooks, where she contemplates creative work from the inside; in her essays she is more likely to look upon art and artists from on high. This fluctuation in her point of view (the view of one who wanted only to be rid of a point of view) leads to some apparent contradictions that perhaps disguise the extent to which her philosophical inquiry is truly close in spirit to a poetic one, even as its scope is much wider.

It is not on the surface that the most significant moral considerations in art lie. There is something in the process of artistic creation that eradicates the superficial elements of the personality and so ensures an unmitigated experience of the creative impulse; there is no hiding: "To let oneself be annihilated right down to some last atom, from the survival (resistance) of which will grow—a world" (152). This is Tsvetaeva's account of the moment of inspiration, which she calls the "[v]isitation of the elemental" (151). John Berryman speaks of something similar, though with less felicity, when he says that luck for the writer consists in being struck in life by that which will almost, but not quite, destroy him. None of this is far removed from Weil's assertion: "Why should I attach much importance to that part of my intelligence that anyone . . . can take away from me? . . . If there is some other thing that proves irreducible, it is that which is infinitely precious" (*VSW* 568). The poet risks being overwhelmed in the service of a creative gift; he or she unreservedly submits. Weil, writing from Marseilles in 1941, can contemplate the possibility of being destroyed by a brutal reality; any surviving particle will serve, not art, but the truth to which she has devoted her whole intellect. The processes are in a sense similar (witness Weil's prayer); the spheres are distinct. Poet and philosopher obey different forces, and it is their response that constitutes action in the moral sphere.

Weil is ultimately a student of Pascal, who knows that the self cannot be relied upon:

And suppose I was loved for my judgment, for my memory, would I, myself, be loved? No, for I can lose these qualities without losing myself. Where then is this self, if it is neither in the body, nor in the soul? And how to love the body or soul if not for these qualities, which are not what constitute the self, since they are perishable? (1165)

What we call the self is a constellation of attributes, all accidental in nature and conveniently hiding our hollowness. We cannot truly expect to bring forth anything worthwhile or anything new (Weil believes this emphatically): "WE MUST IMITATE THE ACT OF

CREATION, AND THERE ARE TWO WAYS OF DOING SO, ONE REAL AND THE OTHER APPARENT: PRESERVATION AND DE-STRUCTION. THERE IS NO TRACE OF 'I' IN PRESERVATION. THERE IS ONE IN DESTRUCTION. 'I' LEAVES ITS MARK ON THE WORLD BY DESTROYING" (*OC* 6:2:256–57). Although Weil's mysticism takes her into different territory from the poet's, the essential observation she and Tsvetaeva both make is that integrity (wholeness) in creation consists in knowingly dispensing with the self with all its defenses and subterfuges, in simply—although it is not simple—allowing the destruction of that self to occur. Only then can one receive the full impact of the poetic visitation; only then can one hope to overcome the deceptive power of the self. Creativity (such as we are capable of) in its inception involves a moral choice. In the case of writing, it is not a question of weighing one's words or images, of premeditating their effect, but of accommodating oneself to the circumstances that will give them weight and freedom.

Weil, of course, understands this; it is she who readily absolves François Villon of his putative life of crime: "What does it matter if Villon was a thief? The act of stealing was, on his part, perhaps a result of need, perhaps a sin, but not an aimless or gratuitous act" ("Lettre aux *Cahiers du Sud*" 357). But she will often speak from the vantage point of the moralist surveying a field. She therefore reminds us that "[e]very activity is related to good and evil in two ways, in its execution and in its principle. A book can therefore be well or poorly written on the one hand and originate either in good or in evil on the other" (*ML* 350). This is a truth more of observation than experience, perhaps; the dismissal of ambiguity, the exclusion of forces in which moral choice is not possible or fully conscious or relevant (rhythm, recourse to memory, obsessive imagery, etc.) suggest a sense of purpose and a degree of self-possession in the writing that not all writers would claim, or even want, to have. In fact, it is perhaps this all-too-willed allegiance to the good that clips the wings of Weil's poetic and dramatic writings, even as her prose so often soars. But she is only interested in one kind of writing, that marked by "a genius of the very first rank in full bloom" (*ML* 351). A writer, however, has simply to work with the poor material at hand. Tsvetaeva concludes her analysis of Pushkin's drama, *Feast in a Time of Plague*, in which she concentrates on the evil figure of

Walsingham, by saying: "The poet perishes when he renounces the elemental. He might as well cut his wrists without ado" (155). And more drolly, or simply with resignation: "Thank the Lord the poet has the hero, the third person—*him*—as a way out. Otherwise, what a shameful (and uninterrupted) confession. Thus, at least the appearance is saved" (155).

It comes as no surprise to Weil's dedicated reader that in Shakespeare it is King Lear, and not Richard III, who captures her imagination—and that fact is instructive. The aspirations she holds dear cannot easily be reconciled to art's worldliness. Tsvetaeva explains it best:

> Artistic creation is in some cases a sort of atrophy of conscience—more than that: a necessary atrophy of conscience, the moral flaw without which art cannot exist. In order to be good (not lead into temptation the little ones of this world), art would have to renounce a fair half of its whole self. The only way for art to be wittingly good is—not to be. It will end with the life of the planet. (157)

She is not arguing that the artist is exempt from responsibility for what is written, only that as an artist sometimes one cannot proceed otherwise. Weil would never admit into her thought relaxation of the moral law in art's behalf; such a regression this would strike her as degrading and contradictory, and as a form of trafficking with the enemy utterly unknown to her exemplary figures. (She was not above this sort of thing herself, however, when it came to the proposal for the front-line nurses.) Philosophically the idealist, she cannot conceive of writing on such terms. When she alludes to "the immorality of letters" (*ML* 352), it is to condemn the general factitiousness of current fiction as the tell-tale evidence of second-rate work and, in the absence of contemporary writers of genius, to advocate rereading the great works of the past.

It is clear from the polemical "Morale et littérature" and "Lettre aux *Cahiers du Sud* sur les responsabilités de la littérature" that Weil had given up on the literary establishment of her day—and her day being that of the Occupation, it is unexceptionable that she had. Her own experience with the publication of her essay on factory work must have been distasteful, despite the good intentions urging it; the general climate surely drove her to believe that literary business as usual could not suffice in the present emergency, if indeed it ever did suffice, morally speaking. Tsvetaeva, writing before the war but already in exile in Paris, seeks to give clarification to something that is very precious—and imperiled. She will defend literature to her last breath, and says so. Weil will instead salvage her beloved works of Homer, Sophocles, Shakespeare, and Racine, and battle her way past the imagination to the truth:

> Imagination on the one hand proceeds to fill vacuums, on the other hand is bound to the present situation; sometimes moves back and forth between these two conditions. Wherever it can meet needs without restrictions, one is at ease. . . . It's agreeable. It invents virtues for the mighty, crimes for the unfortunate. Or the opposite. . . . (Fictional misfortune summons up the image of virtue, and real misfortune that of crime or at least of worthlessness.)
>
> Unease, when the imagination is bound by reality in its efforts of invention. When the conflict is a violent one, feeling of "impossibility." (Impossible that one must die before seeing the morning sun. . . .)
>
> The beautiful: stop put to the lying imagination. (OC 6:2:290)

Weil clearly sees through the mechanism by which we create fictions in our own minds and which, as if by arrangement (our duplicity), in the wake of interruption, lets us fall back quickly "into the demislumber of our chattering" (ML 351). On this subject there is no deceiving her; she knows all the tricks of mindlessness, toward which we gravitate, complacently: "Usually our imagination puts words into noises, in the way the mind lazily plays at seeing forms in wrinkled laundry or smoke" (C 3:274). She is quick to perceive the pleasurable aspect of this debased projection serving as a smokescreen to hide mortality from view; Weil is not so unfamiliar with Baudelaire's universe, after all. Before them both, Pascal understood the temptation: "But diversion keeps us amused and brings us imperceptibly along to our death" (1147). The beautiful exists, Weil says, when we finally stop lying to ourselves; but who can bear to do this?

Writers who only replicate this anesthetizing game earn Weil's contempt; praising those rare writers who can manage to awaken us to the truth (*ML* 351), she would wholeheartedly concur with Kafka's affirmation: "Literature is an axe for the frozen sea within us." In fact, the axe rarely strikes, and Weil has little faith in the source from which it must be forged. Tsvetaeva confirms the reasons for such disenchantment: "[H]ow often in one and the same work, on one and the same page, in one and the same line, they [my works] both release *and* seduce. Like the dubious swill in a witch's cauldron—what *hasn't* been heaped into it and boiled?" (169). Art is by nature impure; Weil insists on purity: "Why give one's heart to anything but the good?" (*E* 297). After all, there are more important things than literature; what defense does the poet have, who must, or who chooses to, go on writing? Unless inspired by the highest degree of genius in full flower, not much of one, according to Weil.

As Joseph Brodsky reminds us, language "is not capable of ethical choice" (56); how can we expect it to be better than we are? Tsvetaeva, with disarming honesty, lays open the whole sordid business of writing a poem, most remarkably in a loving but thoroughgoing dissection of an obscure nun's poem, decidedly not the work of a professional poet (162–64). In the writing of poetry, to its everlasting shame, goodness is a liability: "Knowing the greater, I do the lesser. That is why there is no forgiveness for me" (183). The prospect of entering into such commerce is something from which Weil would recoil in horror, but Tsvetaeva's sense of hierarchy corresponds to her own. Tsvetaeva opens her essay by announcing: "[W]hat I say is addressed exclusively to those for whom God— sin—holiness—*are*" (149). The impulse to write, acted upon, is perhaps an acknowledgment of one's inadequacy to silence; not to hear ourselves would be terrifying—annihilation, fully, or, for the mystic, prayer.

For Weil, the Platonist, writing is translation: "Writing—like translating—negative—pushing away those words that obscure the model, the silent thing that must be expressed" (*OC* 6:1:302). Her poem "Nécessité" seems above all the skillful expression of a concept fully developed before the writing of the poem, a static, secondary event. But the sheer massiveness, the sheer intensity of her work taken as a whole suggest no deadening remove from the ache of injustice. The weight of language, the burden of speech is itself a necessity keenly felt, bitterly questioned, an anguish underlying that immense production: The stars do not respond, and yet what do we have, if not words, to speak of urgent things? If one is writing for the deaf (the remote stars, the Free French who will not let one go on a mission), words are pointless; and what assurance is there that they will have any resonance for posterity, if there is to be a posterity? Why must we always break our silence if, or is it because, God will not break his?

It is to the brink of this silence that Weil's work takes us, and we turn gratefully to the poets to take us back down to our human noise; where we can still, with Beckett and Dickinson, register shock or dismay at the scandal of our abandonment in the universe; where we can continue to delight in those ink-scored objects made to our measure. Before leaving Weil as she moves beyond the threshold at the end of poetry, its art consigned, as Tsvetaeva says, to "that first, lowest sky of the spirit" (167), let us compare a passage from her Marseilles notebooks (*OC* 6:2:104–6) and one from "Art in the Light of Conscience" (172–74) that speak eloquently to our condition as readers and purveyors of words.

The passage from Weil is in some ways a return to the beginning of the Marseilles notebooks, another appraisal of the changed moral and physical landscape. Whereas the first response in the wake of a disaster is to establish one's exact relation to the new reality, to reconnect sentience with consciousness, to overcome one's numbness and begin to read again—this is the essence of her initial survey, complete with analysis of a German uniform—here a delayed course of action, one unfortunately familiar enough, is laid open to inspection:

> READING. Evil, different reading. Passage from evil to the good, like turning a book upside down.
>
> On the non-supernatural level, society is what keeps evil (certain kinds of evil) separate as though by a barrier; a group of criminals or perverts, even if composed of only a few men, removes that barrier.
>
> But what makes one enter into such a group? Either need or thoughtlessness or, more often, a mixture of both; one doesn't think one is committed to it, because *one doesn't know* that, outside the supernatural, society *alone* keeps one from falling naturally into the most atrocious kinds of vice or crime. One

doesn't know that one is becoming something different, because one doesn't know the extent to which one might be changed within by external forces. One always commits oneself without knowing it. (*OC* 6:2:104)

In her observation of a society indeed turned upside down by military occupation, Weil recalls that social restraints in general—nonsupernatural ones, as she would say—create a false sense of freedom, an artifice unmasked in time of war. We perceive the change, but we misread its cause. License is an already present licentiousness, unpent. The image of the open book—any book whatsoever, not excluding the Bible with its ten commandments?—allows one readily to grasp the contrast between the unchanging, codified text (the moral law) and the arbitrariness of the interpretation; one thinks: if only someone would realize how easily the situation might be rectified. Although the focus is on a specific group, "a group of criminals or perverts," the metaphor brings the subject of criminality uncomfortably close to hand.

Weil's sense of the collective responsibility for the French armistice with Nazi Germany precludes the response of simplistic patriotic indignation: if only the Nazis and collaborationists could be removed from power, the great book of French society could be turned around and read aright. There is no great book of French society—otherwise, that society would not have been so easily defeated—and the barriers that were supposed to keep invaders out crumbled from within. Had there been no inner corruption, there would be no complicity now. Lack of self-knowledge is the gateway to moral lapse. Collaboration in evil is a result of the failure to recognize the fragility of civilization; it is not only that a criminal society commits atrocious wrongs, but that it had always been but a hair's breadth away from committing them. Hence we who live complacently are always engaged, even if we had thought to maintain a certain distance from the evil surrounding us. It is a bargain struck within the mind and underwritten by it, sealed by the failure to confront zones of ignorance. Our mental barriers function as do the social ones; they prevent us from seeing the truth about ourselves, and so we have no virtue; when they have fallen, we do not suddenly change our nature, although we may not recognize as our own the viciousness that had previously been submerged. Weil further specifies:

Even to let the imagination linger over certain things as possible (which is completely different from clearly conceiving a
possibility, a thing essential to virtue) is already to commit
oneself. Curiosity is the cause of this. To forbid (not from conceiving, but from lingering over) certain thoughts; not to think
about. People believe that thought doesn't commit one, but it
alone does commit one, and the license of thought imprisons all
freedoms. Not to think about, supreme faculty. Purity, negative
virtue. If what is supreme can be expressed in our language
only by means of negation, in the same way we can imitate it
only by means of negation. Having let the imagination linger
on an evil thing, if one meets other people who make it an
objective reality through their words and actions (when one has
already joined their company) and eliminate the social barrier
in this way, one is already nearly lost. And what could be easier?
No point of rupture; when one catches sight of the ditch, one
has already jumped over it. With the good, it's the opposite; the
ditch is seen at the time of the crossing, at the moment of up-
rooting and being wrenched away. One doesn't fall into the
good. The word "baseness" expresses this property of evil. (*OC*
6:2:104–5)

Complicity in evil begins in the mind, is already accomplished
there in the form of a certain movement of thought that in itself is
an indictment of the undisciplined imagination. Weil does not locate this unbridled force in a Freudian id; the imagination does not
erupt and overflow into ordinary consciousness, distorting perspective and judgment; instead, subject to one's own will—thereby
implicating the dimension of moral choice and with it intellectual
discipline—it is amorphous, hovering indefinitely over possibilities
among which the mind refuses to distinguish, filling the mental
vacuum allowed to exist. The relaxation of moral constraints (thinking about an evil thing) and of intellectual probity (indulging in
consideration of possibilities without intending to make discriminations) amounts to an abdication of conscience, at which point
gravity—falling into evil—takes over. Evil is double-minded in this
view reminiscent of Kierkegaard; just as we might later on find
others only too happy to enter into collusion with us to give the
imagination sway in reality, so already within the mind we know-

ingly give free rein to thoughts that protect us from coming face to
face with the good. The ditch seen after the fact removes all pre-
tense to innocence. What the author of Genesis explains through
narrative Weil presents in terms of a detailed description of the
mind's propensity for compromise.

At this point, Weil's analysis rejoins Tsvetaeva's acknowledgment of the presence, in the act of literary creation, of "a necessary
atrophy of the conscience, the moral flaw without which art cannot
exist" (157); in her view, poetic creation requires the suspension of
thought, as a kind of fluid medium though which ideas and impressions, images and sounds, may freely vie for expression. The
knowing modern artist, engaged by definition in compromise, is no
match for Weil's divinely inspired Homer; Tsvetaeva herself invokes
the example of Tolstoy, who, in later life, turned in moral revulsion
against his own creation (158). In their understanding of the implication of the moral sense in the exercise of the imagination, Weil
and Tsvetaeva speak nearly as one, and their common method—
introspection, augmented by observation—almost seems to proceed
from shared conviction, perhaps originating in a religious sensibility, although in each case one very differently constituted and realized. Tsvetaeva insists on the poet's voluntary subjection to a
dreamlike state:

> The condition of creation is a condition of entrancement. Till you
> begin—*obsession*; till you finish—*possession*. Something, someone,
> lodges in you; your hand is the fulfiller not of you but of *it*. Who
> is this *it*? That which through you wants to be. . . .
>
> The condition of creation is a condition of dreaming, when
> suddenly, obeying an unknown necessity, you set fire to a house
> or push your friend off a mountain-top. Is it your act? Clearly
> it *is* yours (after all, it is you sleeping, *dreaming!*). Yours—in
> complete freedom. An act of yourself without conscience, your-
> self as nature. (172–73)

Obsession, possession, dreaming—this is the book turned upside
down, the waking consciousness abandoned, the self inhabited by
forces social barriers serve to repress, some clamoring for expression
through destruction, others through poetry. Where Weil observes of
the evildoer that "[o]ne doesn't know that one is becoming something

different," attributing his or her fall to lack of self-knowledge, Tsvetaeva asserts—confesses—that the poet does indeed know that something different is coming into being through this process and freely consents to it. The evildoer in Weil becomes aware of the line he or she has crossed only after it is too late; the poet knows the boundary ahead of time, according to Tsvetaeva, yet writes the poem: "Vainly I say to myself: I won't go in (through the door), I won't look (through the window)—I know that I shall go in, and even while I'm saying I won't look, I am looking" (173). This is the same kind of exquisite, unsparing self-awareness we see in Weil when she admits, after writing her "example of a prayer": "But all these spiritual phenomena are absolutely beyond my competence. I know nothing of them. . . . I'm speaking off the top of my head. And I'm not even capable of telling myself sincerely that I'm speaking off the top of my head" (CS 205–6). The poet does not "not think about"—and therein lies her doom. For, as Weil says: "People believe that thought doesn't commit one, but it alone does commit one." Simply to understand, according to Tsvetaeva, is something akin to transgression (in Weil's words again: "No point of rupture; when one catches sight of the ditch, one has already jumped over it."):

> [T]he poems themselves are a key to understanding everything. But from understanding to accepting there isn't just a step, there is no step at all; to understand is to accept, there is no other understanding, any other understanding is non-understanding. Not in vain does the French *comprendre* mean both 'understand' and 'encompass'—that is, 'accept' and 'include.' (173)

Tsvetaeva's poet is not Promethean after Weil's ideal, bringing redeeming light; she is more protozoan—englobing, primitive, reactive—but because endowed with that spark of conscience, irredeemably responsible. She will take everything in. Not so Weil, as she explains in a letter to Father Perrin: "If my eternal salvation were set before me on this table, and if I had only to reach my hand out to obtain it, I would not reach out for so long a time as I thought I had not received the order to do so" (AD 29). "[T]his table" being quite literally Weil's writing table, her imagination of a scene from her intellectual life, into which enters temptation in the guise of an intangible (spiritual) fruit, is far closer to the wellsprings of poetic creation as described by Tsvetaeva than to the sacrificial gesture of her early poem "Prométhée" (*P* 22–24). But here the resemblance ends. Weil is waiting for her orders; the hierarchy is intact. (Or is it that here at this table, for certain, she is the supreme authority, and no one may intrude—with one possible exception.) She absolutely will not be drawn into the orbit of obtrusive desire. That this thought impinges on her at the very moment she is writing—the imagined bait, accidentally glimpsed; the moral necessity of maintaining distance (in its implicit dynamics, a recapitulation of the "Prologue")—seems to establish a connection, one not necessarily oblique, between the outpouring of her later writing and her inability to put down religious or spiritual roots. She must concentrate on her writing; that is the task at hand; she is in her place; there is no other place for her.

Tsvetaeva is equally possessive of her territory: "Find me a poet without a Pugachov [leader of a peasant rebellion]! without an Impostor! Without a Corsican [Napoleon]!—*within*. A poet might lack the power (the means) for a Pugachov, that's all. *Mais l'intention y est toujours*" (174). The intention is always there; the tyrant is just under the surface.

Under the surface lies our true nature, and the poet dives down:

In this realm the poet can have only one prayer: not to understand the unacceptable—let me not understand, so that I may not be seduced. The sole prayer of the poet is not to hear the voices: let me not hear, so that I may not answer. For to hear, for the poet, is already to answer, and to answer is already to affirm, if only by the passionateness of his denial. The poet's only prayer is a prayer for deafness. Otherwise there is the most difficult task of choosing what to hear according to its quality; that is, of choosing the forcible stopping of his own ears to a number of calls, which are invariably the stronger. Choice from birth, that is, to hear only what is important, is a blessing bestowed on almost no one. (174)

"[W]ill, reason, conscience" (174) are the barriers we erect to limit our own capacity for evil; but the poet, who would be accessible to the elemental, takes the barriers down. How fitting that Tsvetaeva should have written a version of *The Pied Piper of Hamelin* (1925): if we want music (poetry) to act as a charm to ward off the evils around us, then we must pay the piper. For the poet, the cost is indiscriminate hearing: the discovery that the ditch has already been jumped over, it is the canal of the inner ear. Tsvetaeva says simply: "Knowing the greater, I do the lesser. That is why there is no forgiveness for me" (183). In the swagger of Baudelaire's *flâneur* one detects the same frank acknowledgment of the nature of the art; there will be no special pleading on Judgment Day.

Weil, who believes in the possibility of purification (decreation), also believes that art and artist can be redeemed; she would have the poet be perfect as the saint is perfect: "Only a perfectly just man could write the *Iliad*" (CS 307). Tsvetaeva would not subscribe to such a confusion of separate realms. The poet, fully conscious of her powers, proudly stands apart. She who affirms that, "In order to be good (not lead into temptation the little ones of this world), art would have to renounce a fair half of its whole self" (157), also says of her fellow human beings: "I allow no one the right of judgment over a poet. Because no one knows" (181). And Weil, who confides something similar to Pétrement, would not judge her: "It isn't that I feel within myself a capacity for intellectual creation. But I do feel obligations connected with such creation. I am not to blame. I can't help it. . . . The conditions of intellectual or artistic creation are such intimate and secret things that no one can understand them from the outside" (AD 65–66).

As these meditations on the mind's encounter with its darkness conclude, a scene from Homer comes to the fore. Tsvetaeva adds this parenthesis:

> (On Odysseus' ship there was neither hero nor poet. A hero is one who will stand firm even when not tied down, stand firm even without wax stuck in his ears; a poet is one who will fling himself forward even when tied down, who will hear even with wax in his ears, that is—once again—fling himself forward.
>
> The only things non-understood by the poet from birth are the half-measures of the rope and the wax.) (174)

Suddenly we are transported from the inner sanctum of the poet's consciousness ("the poet can only have one prayer: not to understand the unacceptable") to the very source of Western literature, to that which is embedded deep within that poetic consciousness— and it is as if, in both instances, we are assisting at a birth: the birth of a poem, the birth of a tradition of poetry. And the impression is not mistaken, for not only does Tsvetaeva refer to the birthright of the poet, but her theme is one of infant vulnerability: the helplessness of hearing. The song of the Sirens is a charm (from the Latin *carmen*, song) intended to lure sailors to their doom, and this music of deception will inevitably seduce the poet, who "will fling himself down"—that is, knowingly and without hesitation, fall into evil, jump over the ditch, travel inside the mind to moral shipwreck if such is the will of the "*it*" that demands expression. The poet is not a hero, only "a definite and invariable mental-artistic reflex" (170). In Tsvetaeva, the conscience of the *poète maudit* undergoes self-examination in the unforgiving light of a religious sense of right and wrong, and there is no equivocating; the exposure of the mental processes of poetic creation that results is devoid of self-pity and flatters no one. And yet, in her experience, that is how poetry is written, or rather, born.

Had Weil read Tsvetaeva's profound and unapologetic essay, she would probably still have offered this interpretation consistent with her reverence for the Ancient Greeks:

> *To conceive the notion and possibility of evil without imagining it; this is what is meant by Ulysses tied to the mast and his sailors with their ears filled with wax.*
>
> Such is not the case (?) with the good. If one conceives it clearly, and if one conceives the possibility of it clearly, one does it. Such is the grace given to man.
>
> *This difference is a criterion of the good (?), a criterion to be applied only if one knows what it is to conceive of something without imagining it.* [READINGS.]
>
> Artists. A human being gifted in an art achieves a degree of excellence in it *exactly* proportional to his ability not to think about.
>
> Similarly for this art that is life itself. (*OC* 6:2:105–6)

Ulysses' ruse, the adoption of those "half-measures" incomprehensible to Tsvetaeva's poet, gives proof of self-knowledge; the hero cultivates self-discipline. The vessel of the mind steers past the source of song, having provided the necessary barriers to evil action (rope, wax). The mind sails clear when it refuses to listen to the deceptive music of the imagination bearing us secretly to our death. The siren song is our own song—false, incessant, noxious:

> In the absence of a heroic love for the truth, we tell stories about our past, revising it to suit our taste. We don't observe others; we tell ourselves what they're thinking, saying, doing. Reality gives us elements, in the way novelists often find their subject in a given event, but we wrap a fog around them in which values are turned upside down as in any fiction, where evil ropes us in and the good is boring. (*ML* 350–51)

In Weil's meditation, this wonderfully apt evocation of the *Odyssey* arises like a triumphant rejoinder to the commonplace image of the ditch introduced early on; the illustrations correspond perfectly in character and register to the contrast between real, not fictional, good and evil she is establishing. The literary and the pedestrian, the noble and the squalid, the high and the low: the artfulness of the opposition is an instance of the poetic thinking that continually lifts Weil's prose out of the ordinary and makes of it a thing inspired. But for her, intent on mastering the art of "not thinking about," not to mention "this art that is life itself," poetry alone is not a sufficient art. That is the truth-seeker's prerogative. Tsvetaeva's assertion, "All the lessons we derive from art, *we* put into it" (156), would no doubt shock and dismay her. She would not turn the book around for *that*. Those who would understand her journey, step by step, word by word, know the stakes are much greater; that Weil carries poetry with her makes the trail easier to find.

Poetics are necessarily personal, inalienable, the crystallization of one person's experience of the world and artistic practice. Tsvetaeva's searching and regal account of poetic creation, in which she acknowledges the primacy of the moral law in all spheres but her own, reflects her unique encounter with the forces she identifies and a degree of self-knowledge as an artist that probably few could have the strength to bear. Weil's is not a poetics in its own right, only one in relation to a metaphysical view of the universe in which the moral law is always and everywhere absolute. If we return to

Heaney's preoccupation today with the influence of poetry as reg-istered on the scales of reality, we see an adaptation of Weil's teach-ing (or, more accurately, an incorporation of an element of it into an already mature aesthetic) that does introduce considerations of a moral nature into the act of creation. (Heaney surely would not exclude the act of writing from considerations of a poet's life.) For if poets are bound to compare all their efforts—and when, as artists, can they effectively do this but in the process of creation—to that higher "plane of consciousness" already unblocked, cleared in their writing, their moral worthiness is not merely at risk (as in Tsvetaeva, who says the poet is, morally speaking, damned), it is a factor in the production of the poem. Poetic intelligence participates in the moral sphere knowingly and must knowingly struggle toward the light—an evolutionary view. (Tsvetaeva, at the height of her genius, speaks of the journey's precariousness, but the destination is al-ways a poem.) Heaney's view is in some ways analogous to Weil's, and being a poet's view, it also more hopeful. If he injects an ele-ment of righteousness into the poetic sphere, assumes responsibil-ity for a standard (it is useful to remember that he is a public and revered poet, Tsvetaeva one marginalized in her lifetime), he knows that consciousness is a trail to be blazed, attacked again and again, with the assurance of the reality of progress—his "field work." Weil has her "Prologue": indeed, there are higher states of consciousness to which we can accede—but not of our own will, we are entirely at the mercy of impersonal forces, and ordinarily we are banished. In this scheme of things, the pen cannot lead anywhere, and its efforts are ultimately useless. Weil's love of Herbert suggests that for her poetry is like a keepsake (as does her whole *motionless* po-etic art, in contradistinction to her prose)—a reflection, something intact, possibly misshapen, fallen from the skies. It is not our depths she wants to plumb; she tastes the bitterness of earthly exile. Poetry cannot make the leap to the stars ("Nécessité"), let alone to the world beyond—a mystic's reproach to what tradition has deemed the highest of the arts. Growing disenchanted with language, even in the midst of a period of astounding creativity, Weil follows her thought to its logical conclusion, seeking to discover that irreduc-ible particle of the good within by means of self-immolation.

6

The Proposal for Front-Line Nurses

In the fall of 1941, Weil wrote to her brother André in the United States: "As for the particular research [a friend] talked to you about, I am certainly not giving up on it; I think about it more and more; but I'm beginning to wonder whether I wouldn't have more opportunities to undertake it by staying here rather than leaving" (*VSW* 585). Even now, Weil was still able to envision a peaceful life for her parents and herself in a village somewhere in the Marseilles region, a life she would voluntarily abandon to pursue her "research"— significantly, the same term she had used to allude to her projected employment in factories in 1934. When Weil and her parents arrived in New York in early July 1942, she talked at once of going to see President Roosevelt to ask him to authorize her current project and was bitterly disappointed when her brother discouraged her (A. Weil, *Souvenirs*, 188). The script meant to bring her exposure to danger and suffering along with the Allied soldiers was never to be taken seriously by those in a position to act upon it, proving that earlier intuition correct.

The form her intended research was to take Weil outlined in her proposal for front-line nurses, a text she enclosed with a letter dated July 30, 1942, to Maurice Schumann, a friend from her days at the Lycée Henri IV, and now a member of the Free French Forces in London (*EL* 187–95). In her letter, Weil states that she would also accept any secret, and preferably dangerous, mission to France (*EL* 186), an offer repeated in subsequent correspondence. By this time she must have realized, or been convinced by André, that her proposal was not likely to be put into action (A. Weil, "Propos," 19). However, given its importance to her and its projection of a response to the Nazi occupation, the proposal clearly bears the stamp of her "peculiar type of imagination," one so constituted that "the misfortune of France would cause me much more pain from a distance than near at hand" (*EL* 185). This work differs radically from the texts previously considered, all of which also respond to the French misfortune, in that, right from the start, Weil did not intend the written page to be the ultimate vehicle for the thought represented there. Read in light of her letters to Schumann from New York and London and her earlier correspondence with writer Joë Bousquet (April–May 1942), the work provides insight into the spiritual and psychological imperatives underlying it and astonishes by the brilliance of a rhetoric deployed in the service of a transgressive ideal. Weil's vision of the battlefield, and of the use to which it might be put, could only have come from her singular "type of imagination," hurling itself against the French defeat as if daring to be shattered.

The text itself is an impressive display of rhetorical skill and relentlessness intended to disarm any opposition. Weil begins the proposal by citing prior approval for her plan: "The following proposal was the subject of a favorable report by the Senate armed forces committee to the War Ministry in France in 1940. The rapidity of events put any attempt to enact it out of the question" (*EL* 187). Weil allies reason and honor in her cause; appropriate officials have once already recognized the merit of the proposal, and these were legitimate authorities (from before the signing of the armistice). In and of itself, she implies, the plan is compelling and patriotic—that is to say, in view of the continuing emergency, unassailable. The language is resolute and impersonal, focused on the business at hand.

The origins of the proposal go back much further than the date cited. After war had been declared against Germany in 1939, Weil chafed at being behind the front lines, a restless curiosity manifest from her childhood—she had asked directly about the fighting in letters to the family's informally "adopted" soldier during the Great War (*VSW* 26)—and one that had prompted her to join a brigade of anarchists in Spain in 1936, during the civil war. About the latter experience, she was to write to the novelist Georges Bernanos: "I don't love war, but what has always horrified me the most about it is the situation of those behind the front lines" (*VSW* 385). Upon hearing of the brutal suppression by the Nazis of a student uprising in Prague, she wanted to organize a mission, in which she would naturally have taken part, to parachute troops and arms into Czechoslovakia (*VSW* 489). Later, in the first months of 1940, anticipating the German advance, she pinned her hopes on a new plan: the formation of a team of nurses to tend the wounded at the front lines of battle. Having had to bring her back from Spain, following an accident, only several years before, her parents arranged for a senator they knew to meet with her and feign approval of the proposal, if only to distract her from further adventures. Accordingly, Weil thought it had been forwarded to the War Ministry for consideration, when nothing of the sort had happened (*VSW* 512). The cornerstone of her argument, unwittingly laid by worried parents trying to protect her from herself, had no basis in fact.

Weil goes on to present a more recent endorsement:

> Attached is a letter expressing the opinion on this proposal of Joë Bousquet, a veteran of the other war who is severely disabled. Having received an injury to the spinal chord in 1918, and paraplegic as a result, he has not since been able to move. His experience of the war is much closer to him than is the experience of those who resumed a normal life after 1918; moreover, his opinion is that of a mature man. For this reason his is precious advice. (*EL* 187–88)

Weil now rests her argument on the foundation of a veteran's tragic proximity to his experience of an earlier war won by France. From a military standpoint, it might be argued that it was precisely such proximity that made French resistance to the German advance in

1940 wholly ineffective. But the proposal has already entered into the realm of Weil's religious metaphysics, governed by a different perspective. That Weil attributes to the state of immobility access to the truth itself—a belief summed up in images such as that of the fallen master in the snow rescued by means of beauty's urgent call ("La Personne et le sacré"), of the shell of the ruined self now occupied by an all-encompassing God (the prayer)—is a distinction that in the proposal can perhaps only be gleaned from the intensity of emphasis in her description of Bousquet. Her insistence on the maturity and timeliness of his opinion suggests that he, because of his condition, understands better than most the ordeal France is going through and the moral inspiration it now needs. As she was to write in *L'Enracinement*, any illusion of grandeur has evaporated in the face of the nation's evident fragility: "Compassion for one's country is the only sentiment that does not ring false at this moment, that is appropriate to the condition in which the spirit and flesh of the French people are now found, and that possesses both the humility and the dignity befitting misfortune" (*E* 220–21). Weil is hardly one to merely play on the sympathies of her readers; she evokes Bousquet's paralysis, which for her symbolizes the state of occupied France, by way of establishing his authority. She does not mention his identity as a poet and novelist sharing many of the same spiritual preoccupations as her own, including an interest in the Cathars; the aesthetic and religious dimension of his judgment, of great importance to her, is left to invisibly lend weight to his opinion.

Single-mindedness is a virtue, according to Kierkegaard, and it also can be wearing. This is not the Weil who speaks from on high in "La Personne et le sacré" or who moves unceremoniously into the wrenching experiments of her prayer and her prologue. Supremely conscious of her intended audience, she invokes higher military authority and makes her argument the rhetorical equivalent of an armed offensive, going on to anticipate the material objections to her plan and demolish them one by one. But from the start the proposal is not fully anchored in material reality. Part of the fantastical element of the proposal derives from the detachment of its rhetoric from the deepest part of the motivation underlying it, which was intensely personal and spiritual in nature. That the proposal reached De Gaulle is a tribute to her tenacity and to

Schumann's friendship; the general's exclamation upon reading it—
"She's insane!" (*VSW* 667)—is precisely the reaction she was anticipating and hoped to ward off by speaking in logistical terms. It is
only fair that Weil should have returned the compliment after her
fashion, asserting in a paper that De Gaulle should not tarnish his
place of honor in French history by taking up a political career after
the war (*EL* 71).

Having cited her sources of authority, Weil now introduces her
subject: "This proposal concerns the constitution of a special formation of front-line nurses. This formation would be very mobile and
in principle should always be in the most perilous places in order
to administer 'first aid' [in English in the original text] in the midst
of battle" (*EL* 188). Only ten or even fewer nurses would be needed
to set the plan in motion; it could be executed quickly, as the training
needed is "practically none" (*EL* 188). Identifying volunteers equal to
the task poses no problem: "The horrors of war are today so much
present in everyone's imagination that a woman capable of presenting herself voluntarily for such a purpose might well be regarded as
very probably being capable of carrying it out" (*EL* 188).

The first few pages of the proposal concern the nurses themselves, with emphasis on the status of their mission as an "experiment" or "first trial," for what matters most is that the project be
launched at any cost; Weil would be sure of realizing her ambition,
as she would be a member of the inaugural group. The service the
nurses would render almost appears to be an afterthought, or at
least something incidental, requiring scant attention; indeed, the
same might be said of the soldiers themselves, who appear in an
allusion to a hypothetical breakdown of morals (which would not
happen; she has Bousquet's solemn assurance on this point
[*Correspondance* 34]). Weil minimizes the group and the risk involved;
there would be "a very small core of volunteers," "the drawbacks
are almost nonexistent," "no organization" would be necessary (*EL*
188); indeed, when the time comes to evaluate the effort, "[t]he
experiment having been done on a minuscule scale and without
publicity, there would be no drawback, except for the losses that
might have occurred" (*EL* 189). The argument circles around the
small number of nurses involved, the likelihood of success, the
absence of drawbacks, the ease of canceling the operation in the
event of failure. It is a given that the nurses are expendable, which

is of course a status they would share with the troops: "Generally speaking, there is no reason to consider the life of a woman, especially if she has gone past early adulthood without being a wife or mother, as being more precious than the life of a man; all the more so if she accepts the risk of death" (*EL* 189).

Weil, who declined any association with feminism in her own early adulthood, seeks equality here, at the hands of military men, and she seeks it literally on their own turf. No wonder she tries to make herself and her project seem small. That she crafts the proposal the way she does, expending great effort initially to show that the women themselves are not to be considered an obstacle, reflects her expectation that her readers will be horrified at the notion of allowing women on the battlefield at all. Casting them in a supportive role may well have seemed to her the only way to get around a wall of prejudice. As Margaret Collins Weitz concludes from her interviews with Weil's female contemporaries: "French women who wanted to join military or paramilitary organizations were not accepted readily. Charles de Gaulle was a traditional military leader who had difficulty envisioning women in combat" (147). And gaining access to the battlefield is all-important to Weil; there is no question of volunteering to nurse behind the lines at a field hospital, under supervision. Her nurses stand ready to be deployed to "the roughest places, to run as great a risk as the soldiers in the most danger, or an even greater risk than theirs, and doing so without the support of the spirit of being on the offensive, but instead bending over the injured and dying" (*EL* 189). Death would be almost certain. That Weil turned for support to a stranger, Joë Bousquet, whom she met only in early April 1942, rather than to her own father, who had been an army doctor in the same war, needs no explanation. At the same time, as Nevin notes in his analysis of the text, there is an element of poetic justice, a certain wishfulness, in all of this: "In the nurse's anonymous calling, she could have found a *revanche* [revenge] for the cruel fate that made her as a woman an outsider, and she would have remembered that in the Great War France had accepted and acknowledged the sacrificial services of its Jews" (190). Weil will be at home here, in a setting from which only death can expel her and where the danger she seeks will be hers.

Indeed, so set is her conception of this project that, however immediate and profound their friendship, Weil largely ignores Bousquet's advice. In response to her questions—it is almost as if she is reviving the earlier correspondence with the "adopted" soldier of her childhood—he tells her of the Allied women nurses and ambulance drivers he had once seen at the front in 1918, writing admiringly of the assurance and dispatch with which they removed the wounded from the field after the fighting had suddenly overrun their station. He is troubled by the static image she appears to have of military operations: "You seemed to expect that the women intending to provide moral comfort to the wounded would remain indefinitely on the battlefield, without ever being relieved. That is a romantic and impractical idea" (*Correspondance* 35). He recommends that she revise her proposal to allow for the attachment of the nurses to a particular outfit.

But Weil clings to her own vision. She concludes this first part of the proposal almost triumphantly: "In this way, the objections that come to mind at the first sight of such a proposal are reduced to very little, one might say to nearly nothing, upon careful examination. To the contrary, the advantages are all the more obvious and seem all the greater when one examines them more closely" (*EL* 190). It is as though she is switching lenses on a microscope; if we keep on looking into the eyepiece we will surely see what Weil sees. She then expends all of two paragraphs on the actual care the soldiers might hope to receive—another advantage of the plan "counterbalanced by practically no drawback at all" (*EL* 190)—and then moves on to the part of the argument that interests her most, the one pertaining to the moral and symbolic dimension of the action she desires to accomplish.

Weil has already traversed the battlefield in her imagination in her majestic essay "L'*Iliade* ou le poème de la force," written in 1938 or 1939. Of the exercise of power, or might, she says there:

[I]t petrifies in different ways, but still equally, the souls of those subjected to it and the souls of those who wield it. . . . Battles are not decided by men who calculate, plan, resolve to do something and carry it out, but among men stripped of these faculties, changed, fallen to the level either of inert matter that is merely passive, or of blind forces that are mere bursts of energy. . . . The thoughtlessness of those who heedlessly manipulate the men and the things they have or think they have at their mercy, the despair that compels the soldier to destroy, the crushing of the slave and the vanquished, the massacres—all of these combine to create a uniform image of horror. Might is its sole hero. A dreary monotony would result from this were it not for the presence, scattered here and there, of luminous moments, brief and divine moments in which men have a soul. (*OC* 2:3:245–46)

As Alfred Kazin reminds us, to compare this vision extracted from Homer's text to the original work is to miss "the real subject of the piece: Hitler's war" (96). Similarly inspired, Weil's exercise in prayer, derived from John of the Cross, stares down the realistic possibility of sudden annihilation. Her proposal for the nurses is in effect a transposition of this war scene from the *Iliad*, the nurses embodying those "luminous moments" miraculously interspersed in the darkness. This new tableau will be churned up and destroyed in its turn, added to the appalling waste of war. But whereas those moments are presented as fortuitous in nature in the *Iliad*, the proposal is designed in such a way as to force them to occur, to engineer their presence. Once this has happened, according to Weil's philosophy, there is something certain to be gleaned; she tells Bousquet:

Once outside the egg, you will know the reality of war, the most precious reality to be known, because war is unreality itself. To know the reality of war . . . is the fullness of the knowledge of the real. That is why you are infinitely privileged, for you have war residing permanently in your body. . . . Happy are they for whom the misfortune penetrating their body is also the misfortune of the world itself in their time. They have the ability and the function to know the misfortune of the world in truth. (*Correspondance* 38–40)

Weil's beatitude—so far removed in spirit from Pascal's modest elucidation of the thirst for righteousness' sake—would supply the meaning of those soul-filled moments generally absent from her picture of the *Iliad*. She speaks of a knowledge gained only through experience (conveyed by the French verb *connaître*, to know) in tones reminiscent of her remark, addressed to Father Perrin, of only a few days later: "[E]ach time I think of the crucifixion of Christ, I commit the sin of envy" (*AD* 62). It is somewhat disconcerting to see her tell Bousquet, after his many years of paralysis, that the knowledge of war's reality will one day be his. She adopts the role of spiritual adviser, and at the same time she exposes her lack of the one thing needful for ultimate authority, that "fullness of the knowledge of the real." A compassionate interpreter of the mechanisms of suffering represented in the *Iliad*, she is ready now to transport herself bodily to a corresponding setting; the trajectory from reader to actor is implicit.

If the written page is no longer able to contain Weil's aspirations, she will go on write many more of them, languishing in New York and relegated to a desk job in London. Even if that page is "an object made to our measure" (*C* 3:162), Weil no longer wants our measure; she will deal in absolutes. With the proposal for the nurses as her chosen instrument, Weil would force an opening where she could pass into the unknown, the inexpressible. In its originality, her method is indeed akin to poetry of the era; in the words of novelist Elsa Triolet, "To create these works of art which attacked and undermined the Occupation, it was necessary to invent new forms and new contents in which to clothe the spirit of the Resistance. There were no rules and no theories: each artist had to create his own, forged from his own art" (Weitz viii). In its sheer outrageousness, her method has something of poetry's inherent excess. According to Tsvetaeva: "For one thing, a poet is someone who goes beyond the soul's bounds. A poet is *out* of his soul, not *in* it—his very soul *is* the being out! For another, he goes beyond the soul's bounds—in words" (48). It is the latter condition that identifies the poet, through language still close to the world; Weil would dispense with even that link, too much like the shell she imagines Bousquet breaking out of. Her projected book, its "Prologue" telling of expulsion, will explode into fragments; her prayer flaunts the unbearable confines of human existence. "Any where out of the world" (1:356), wrote Baudelaire, in English, already beyond the native tongue.

What underlies the proposal as a whole, and most visibly the last part, is Weil's "transgressive spirituality" (214), so identified by Oxenhandler in the course of his illuminating comparison of Weil and Michel Foucault:

> During this period in 1942 Weil entered that madness that for Foucault places the transgressor outside the social context and makes him or her a pariah. . . . Madness or delusion is not, for Foucault, a question of truth content or congruence with "reality." Madness is thought that transgresses the limits set on discourse by the social order. . . . [It is marked by] the hysterical use of fantasy as a performative path to experiences that remain beyond the boundaries of what can be cognitively known and accepted. . . . [T]here is throughout [Weil's] work a powerful sense of humanity as flawed, distorted, deluded by the weight of its institutions and the lunacy of institutional thinking. Her response was not the humanist's one of improving institutions but, rather, the mystic's impulse to self-sacrifice. . . . This impulse was materially expressed by her year of factory work during which she was transformed. Her emotions took on a new intensity; they were not simply responses to intolerable working conditions but became signs of a mystical process driving beyond the fundamental limits of human existence. (210–11)

Weil's proposal, of course, speaks only of what can be represented, what the spectator of her "tableau" (*EL* 193) might be expected to see. Only on the surface does she appear to be defying conventional wisdom; more profoundly and radically, she has already, long before, dismissed such wisdom and is now vying to move beyond. One of the paradoxes of the text is the combination of the cold precision of its argument—the analytical rigor, the strict impersonality of reference, the implacability of tone—with the desperate personal need of the author. It is as if Weil makes of the proposal a hard object with which to pierce through the barriers of those uninitiated minds who will read it. Having decimated the inevitable objections arising at first glance, having summarized the beneficial effects of the nurses' caretaking, she goes on to impose a reading of the battlefield scene—once again, presupposing the incomprehension of her readers—but it is a superficial reading, a kind of concession. Weil paints a picture for our—for the world's—edification; but she herself would pass through it. The argument shifts and widens, using a telescopic lens where a microscopic one sufficed before, and contradicts much of what came earlier. Having brought the reader this far, she does not turn back. Approval is the goal. "A meal isn't meant to be compared [to other meals]; it is meant to be eaten," she tells Schumann (*EL* 202); a proposal such as this is not meant to be studied for the consistency of its argument, but to be enacted.

In the final pages of her proposal, Weil makes explicit what is implicit in her essay on the *Iliad*, taking on Hitler directly:

Hitler has never lost sight of the essential necessity to strike the imagination of everyone: of his people, of enemy soldiers, and of the conflict's countless spectators. Of his people, in such a way as to ceaselessly press upon them a new impulse to go forward. Of his enemies, in such a way as to incite the greatest possible disturbance among them. Of the spectators, in such a way as to surprise them and make an impression. (*EL* 191)

Now Weil begins to inscribe her proposal in the sphere of propaganda, recognizing the enemy's success in penetrating into the privacy of the mind, into that domain susceptible to art and religion, artificially stimulating action accompanied by brutal reinforcement. She goes on to refer to the effectiveness of the elite military groups such as the SS and the German paratroopers, and soon one realizes where she is heading:

These formations are made up of men chosen for special tasks, ready not only to risk their lives, but to die. That is the essential thing. They are driven by an inspiration different from that of the bulk of the army, an inspiration resembling a faith, a religious spirit. (*EL* 191)

Except for the last observation, this is the same language that Weil uses to describe her group of nurses. She will counter Hitler's masterstroke with a superior one of her own making, restoring balance to the symbolic struggle between good and evil. Her analysis rejoins the longer exposition put forth in "Cette guerre est une guerre de religions" ("This War is a War of Religions"), written in London, where she deplores the European surrender after the First World War to a moral lassitude that has kept it from making "any effort to escape the concentration camps" (*EL* 99). In describing the war in terms of a spiritual crisis, she provides the metaphysical backdrop for her proposal: "Mysticism is the passage beyond the sphere where good and evil are in opposition, and this by the union of the soul with the absolute good" (*EL* 102). The altruism of the nurses springs from a genuine religious spirit; they themselves will represent the good in the lower symbolic order; and ultimately, for those among them so disposed and so gifted (first and foremost their leader), their action will be the passageway to the highest knowledge. Weil cannot speak of the final goal in the context of her proposal, but she can develop an argument confined to the lower sphere.

Having previously insisted on the near invisibility of the nurses, she now presents their action as inseparable from the viewing of it: "[W]hen it comes to striking the imagination, any copy misses the point. Only the new is striking. . . . We must make the new spring forth" (*EL* 191). Her sense of the moral and spiritual ennui into which Europe had fallen seems to contradict, or augur poorly for, this aspiration to pour new wine into old wineskins; where is the "moral vitality" (*EL* 191) so sadly lost to come from? Weil has begun to give her plan a symbolic reading corresponding to its literal purpose, the provision of care for wounded soldiers: it will provide the shock treatment needed also on the spiritual plane by an exhausted civilization. To do this, the action must be seen by others, on the battlefield and in the imagination; the meaning of her words must step out of the written page: "At the front, words must be replaced by acts. The existence of special formations animated by a spirit of total sacrifice constitutes at every moment a propaganda in action" (*EL* 192). The originality of her response to Hitler's brutal elite will disarm them morally and galvanize the Allies. Her allusion to Joan of Arc (*EL* 192) hardly seems misplaced.

Indeed, at this juncture, Weil begins to multiply her references to the feminine presence constituted by her corps of nurses: "the feminine formation proposed here," "these humane services would be carried out by women and enveloped in maternal tenderness," "these women would be few in number," "[a] small group of women," "this feminine corps," "composed of unarmed women" (*EL* 192–93). What had been hidden, or at least made to seem very small, Weil now shouts from the rooftops; the novelty of this deployment of nurses will electrify the general public:

> Its symbolic significance would be grasped everywhere. This corps on one side and the SS on the other would create by their opposition a tableau preferable to any slogan. It would be the most striking representation possible of the two directions between which humanity today is obligated to choose. (*EL* 193)

Weil wishes her readers to see the possibilities for exploiting this visual propaganda in the service of the Allied cause, to make use of it after their manner. The tableau freezes, like a photograph, the clash between opposing moral forces; it pits young men armed for combat against mature life-sustaining women; their uniforms literally create a contrast of black (or gray) and white. The Allied soldiers, the dead, and the wounded have no role to play in this scene. Moral ambiguity is banished; the message to those behind the lines could not be clearer.

The primacy Weil gives the symbolic dimension alerts us once more to the poetic element involved in the creation of this image. It originates deep in the psyche, corresponding to personal, not solely national, need; it is masked by language confined to a meaning intended for the audience, not expressing the desire of the subject. To achieve this, Weil must displace herself from the proposal—not express her deepest motivation—even as she puts herself symbolically, at one with the nurses, at the center of her discourse and her tableau. She is inside the proposal as an object (viewed by the spectator) and outside it, invisibly, as its creator, her presence felt in the oppressive sense of urgency and the unstated goal of transcendence propelling it. As in the "Prologue," the imagined self, under extraordinary circumstances, finds communion— here, in the form of service to injured soldiers—only to be violently ejected, the death by enemy fire being minimized by Weil even more than the feminine presence. Whereas the abandonment to meaninglessness in city streets leaves only vague hope, the near certainty of death promises the only direct revelation one might be certain of ever having. The "Prologue" makes of mystical union a memory; the proposal is to serve as a means of possibly achieving it again. The self is always the obstacle; it persists, uselessly ("Prologue," the prayer), it must be obliterated (the proposal). It hovers around and in the written page, weighing in with the unstated; it appears there obliquely, masked as a character, even if blending into a group. In an undated letter to Schumann written in London, Weil pleads for release from desk work, from writing position papers: her supervisor, André Philip, must, she argues, "put me in the only place where, for a mind like mine, ideas can come forth: in contact with the object" (EL 212). Words have become inauthentic: "It is too easy to risk the most extreme dangers on paper when there is no reason to think any real effect will come out of it. Nothing is more contemptible. How could I not consider myself contemptible?" (EL 214).

Weil was not the only patriotic Frenchwoman who sought assignment to a dangerous mission, prepared to risk all, only to be rebuffed or ignored by De Gaulle's headquarters; as Weitz remarks, "[t]o participate in missions and maneuvers ran counter to traditional, patriarchal wisdom about the role of women in the military" (169). For Weil, who was told her physical type would only spell danger for herself and her colleagues were she to be sent clandestinely to France, the refusal of her service seemed particularly cruel. In her desperation, she assures Schumann of her readiness to divert the enemy and sacrifice herself should a mission run into difficulty. Back in Marseilles, she tells him, where she had been interrogated by French police after distributing Resistance tracts, divine inspiration had helped her maintain her composure: "You understand in this way why the proposal I've made to you—the one of being scapegoat—is easy for me. It implies nothing more than what had been forcefully imposed on me, in any case" (EL 208). Weil could not accept definition of who she was on others' terms, as she made clear in her letter to the Minister of Education, claiming no attachment to her Jewish background. But in her imagination, finding its expression in the glorious language of Racine and Pascal, she runs toward annihilation. There is no earthly way out. In the proposal for the nurses, she is writing a script for a death acceptable to her, one fulfilling her personal vocation; in the face of rejection, she tells Schumann: "The proposal I had sent you would have perfectly met my needs in this regard" (EL 200). Her needs, too, are divinely inspired: "I think I have the command from God to undertake to prove by experience that [the thoughts sent to her from above] are not incompatible with an extreme form of warlike action" (*EL* 203). Finally, she provides the gloss of her proposal:

> I am being ripped apart, more and more, both in the intellect and at the center of my heart, by the inability to hold together in my mind, in the light of truth, the misery of men, the perfection of God, and the link between the two.
>
> I have the inner certainty that this truth, if it is ever given to me, will be so only in the moment when I myself will be physically in misery, and in one of the extreme forms of the present misery. (*EL* 213)

The moment of extinction links heaven and earth in truth that she will momentarily possess. The tableau she has imagined is meant to be obliterated, giving life its brief, redeeming meaning, its "luminous moment."

But in her proposal, Weil's imagination does not linger on what might be the nurses' own perspective as they tend to the wounded and dying. She turns instead to the effect their presence would have on the young soldiers, thrust into an atmosphere of violence and far from home:

> what could be better than to let them be accompanied even under fire, even in scenes of the greatest brutality, by something that constitutes a living evocation of the homes they have had to leave behind, not a tender evocation but, on the contrary, an exalting one? Then there would never be a moment when they had the depressing impression of being cut off from all they love. (*EL* 194)

Although allowing herself, in the last sentence, a confessional aside, Weil would above all appeal to the self-interest of her readers, military men; the presence of her nurses on the battlefield would increase their chances of victory. She is in their camp. And there is historical precedent besides:

> The ancient Germans, those semi-nomadic tribes the Roman armies could never subjugate, recognized the exalting character

of a female presence in the heart of combat. They had the custom of placing a young girl, surrounded by the elite of the
young warriors, at the head of the lines. (*EL* 194)

Weil's source, according to Pétrement (585), is Tacitus; if the
battlefield experience of World War I is already irrelevant to the
present situation, how can one possibly entertain the idea of reviving such an ancient custom? Robert Coles responds to the uninten-
tional comicality of this inspiration, remarking upon the presence
of "a delicious minor irony in the ancient German warrior's life
prompting a dream or two in the modern French woman's mind.
And where did she find this dream but in Tacitus—she who made
such derisive attacks on Rome, never finding anything worthwhile
to say about it or its writers or heroes" (34). Adapting the image,
Weil does not cast herself alone or as a soldier; she makes a virtue
of her few more advanced years (she would have been thirty-one
years old when she first devised the plan), and she will blend into
the group, making herself and her desire inconspicuous, as compared with her more exultant predecessor. For the moment, forgetting that this corps of nurses is the group meant to be witnessed by
the whole world, we are to concentrate on the Allied soldiers and
their motivation.

To conclude her proposal, Weil returns to the problem of re-
cruitment, again nodding to her audience: "There is always the risk
that women might constitute an obstruction if they do not possess
an amount of cold and virile resolve preventing them from thinking
themselves important in any situation whatsoever" (*EL* 195). To get
the job done, the women chosen must be like men, as though courage could not otherwise be theirs. A small group of women possess-
ing both this resolve, naturally resembling the readers' own, as well
as the care-giving capacity of nurses, will come forward; having
minimized their presence at the beginning of her argument, now, of
her own personal authority, Weil minimizes the difficulty of orga-
nizing the formation: "These women most certainly exist. It is easy
to find them" (*EL* 195). And, formally bringing herself into the picture for the first and only time, Weil declares: "It seems impossible
to me to conceive of any other way of putting these few women to
use with greater effectiveness than in such a formation" (*EL* 195).
The economy of war demands their sacrifice; common sense so

dictates, too. Striking a final blow to overcome any resistance on the part of her readers, Weil adds a postscript attesting to the impact of the quick application of shock treatment, based on a recent article from the *Bulletin of the American College of Surgeons*, by her research triumphantly bridging the distance between the ancient Romans and the present day, between exile in the United States and the return to her beloved France.

As in one of Baudelaire's prose poems, the logical edifice carefully constructed here, the appearance of a reasonableness cultivated to appeal to her audience, cannot completely distract from the overall strangeness of the proposed undertaking. Breaking through the surface is the irrepressible self, cast as an indirect object and ultimate authority; as if solving a logistical problem which had been delegated to her—a posture constituting a cruel irony in view of the work she was to be given in London—Weil indicates that she has found the correct answer. But the point of departure of the proposal is neither the need for emergency shock treatment on the battlefield nor the exploitation of the particular resources of individuals; Weil's preoccupation throughout, on the level of argument as well as in theme, has been with the foundation of authority for a firmly held scheme, depicted as a symbolic opposition to be acted out and publicly interpreted. The ring of certainty and triumph in the conclusion jars with the tentativeness of much of Weil's exposition, which does not lead inexorably to the conclusion that this formation is the only use conceivable for certain languishing supporters of the Allied cause; if anything, the evidence points to this idea's having necessarily originated in Weil's imagination. No one claiming to be reasonable would dispute her closing sentiment— "And our struggle is so hard, so vital, that, as much as possible, each human being must be used with the maximum effectiveness" (*EL* 195)—but there was nothing reasonable about the proposal or the conditions prompting its creation. The defensive posture Weil adopts from the start anticipates the reader's impulse of rejection, the arbitrary cruelty of powers unjustly over her—a situation in some ways not unlike the one she had left behind in Vichy France. The tension between convention and the self visible in the proposal—in the cold, bureaucratically inspired language adopted to argue a cause passionately espoused; in the supportive role assigned a female corps intended to invade the masculine preserve of the battlefield; in the construct of a proposal whose most compelling motivation must remain concealed—seems to break in that single personal reference, "It seems impossible for me to conceive of any other way"—shattering in a way not obvious on the surface, where the reference merely seems inconsistent, but still perceptible in this final plea for recognition transcending considerations of the author's person.

The forced restraint of Weil's rhetoric, here and elsewhere, is one source of its power. As Oxenhandler observes, "Interdiction weighed on Weil, this inability to say whatever she liked, to speak from the heart. It was internalized, largely self-imposed; in her *Journals* we find it constantly coming into play. The transgressor's strength comes from the fact that she has internalized the taboo yet overcomes it anyway" (213). In the proposal, where if she is to reach her audience, Weil must deliberately cultivate an attitude and rhetoric at variance from her deepest thoughts and emotions, interdiction is apparent, as is the desired transgression; but if the inability to speak freely is something internalized—and probably on some level conscious, as is plainly the case here, if less so in the notebooks—it is also something reinforced by powerful social and political forces. If much of one's world seems bent on one's extermination, let alone the denial of one's usefulness because of prejudice, what distance must one travel within to find that free and authentic voice to claim as one's own? Weil's struggle to incorporate different kinds of rhetoric and narrative into her later writings, a struggle meeting varying degrees of success, and sometimes none at all, is set in a context where her speech itself is a transgression, because the very fact of her existence is a transgression—whether so viewed from the worldly perspective of a Talleyrand or Hitler, or from the perspective of her religious metaphysics, the product of her search for the truth. The troubling congruence of the two, which is at the center of much of the criticism and condescension directed toward her, may well have killed her desire to go on living, or caused her to despair of progressing spiritually, unable to hold together in her mind "the misery of men, the perfection of God, and the link between the two" (*EL* 213). Certainly her insistence in the final paragraphs of "La Personne et le sacré" on the talismanic power of words referring to absolutes stems from a conviction that investigations in language at some point reach a dead end. Her faith in these

words is, however, wholly out of tune with her era, and in defer-
ring the highest revelation to the moment of death, when the burden of perspective (not only of seeing, but also of having an
individual voice) is dissolved, she would dispense with language
entirely. In the proposal, where she argues with military men and
takes on the Nazi use of symbolism, we see her in effect trafficking
with the enemy, adapting her language to his, letting material and
the lower moral considerations take precedence over the spiritual
as part of her strategy, and fighting a losing battle.

Weil wanted to test her beliefs, not merely write about them—
which is, of course, why she cannot be classified as merely a poet
or writer. She sought a mystical knowledge distinct from the expression of it, for her of secondary importance. This understanding
of the subsidiary nature of language (recalling the role the team of
nurses, her symbolic instrument, would play) emerges in her correspondence with Bousquet, her most sympathetic reader, to whom
she entrusted, along with an earlier version of her proposal, a draft
of *Venise sauvée*. He enthusiastically tells her:

> I would like to read mystical impressions by you and know how
> you analyze what you experience. . . . I don't fear from you that
> feminine complacency belied by all your aspirations. It is because
> you could never be weak without doing violence to yourself that
> I expect a great deal from a mystical rapture to which you would
> have consented with great difficulty. Think about it; the trite, dis-
> credited subjects are waiting for someone intended, unbeknownst
> to him or her, to reveal their true greatness. You would write some
> truly fine things about divine love. Their charm is practically fore-
> told in your work of violence. . . . (*Correspondance* 27)

Bousquet, poet and writer, would have Weil rescue a kind of literature from obscurity and sentimentality. He seems to associate her
potential with writing Luce Irigaray identifies as *la mystérique*:

> So might be designated that which, in a perspective still remain-
> ing theo-logical, onto-theo-logical, is called mystical discourse or
> speech. Names that are again imposed by consciousness to sig-
> nify that stage beyond, that other stage, *cryptic* to it. Thereby
> indicating the place where it is no longer in control, that "dark

night," but also the fire and flames where it is lost to its extreme confusion. Place where "she" speaks—or he, but through recourse to "she"—of the dazzling effect of the source of light, logically repressed; of the effusion of the "subject" and of the Other in an embrace (conflagration) that confounds them as terms. . . . This place, the only one in the history of the West where woman speaks, acts in such a public way. (238)

The genre for her efforts is prescribed for her by Bousquet, but Weil would not write as a typical "she." Because of her strength and resistance to the overthrow of the intellect, she would bring fresh insight to the field, produce dazzling works, reconquer abandoned territory. On such short acquaintance, Bousquet could not have realized how antipathetic such terms must have seemed to her, for Weil believed it is not literature the writer serves, but the truth. That she did not dismiss his encouragement out of hand is obvious in light of the promptness and urgency of her reply, as well as in the last letters she wrote to Father Perrin and in her "Prologue," although in none of these does she adopt a kind of discourse meant to enter into or speak from the space of mystical ecstasy. She does not attempt to reproduce or repossess it through language, nor is linguistic transgression—venturing into the inexpressible, or merely defying literary convention—her goal. She wants only the direct contact with the object; writing stands in the way, it is a screen, a buffer. In her brutally direct reply to Bousquet, Weil seems to say that the generative force of the works of Pascal and Racine in her writing has played itself out:

To make human readers, by means of imperfect poems, catch a glimpse of the world's beauty such as we sense it underneath its veils—what is such a thing beside the duty to give the world's beauty back naked to God in our death?

"And death, withdrawing clarity from my sight,
Gives back all its purity to once-sullied light."

But if instead of welcoming criminal thoughts like Phèdre, we live innocently, it is in our eyes that the light, sullied by them our whole life long, will find complete purity at the moment of our death.

It is for this reason that I am afraid of death, just as when at a concert I see a great violinist about to make the first strike of the bow when I am not quite ready to listen. It is a joy so great that it must not come prematurely. ("Deux lettres inédites" 140)

Weil's assertion that literary achievement pales beside the far greater spiritual privilege awaiting her at the moment of death seems to rather cruelly put Bousquet in his place, trapped in mere literature (a thought perhaps tinged by Mallarmé), immobilized in a body still withholding that revelation she, in the exaltation of her prose, is rushing forward to embrace. The imperfection of human vision, all too clearly reproduced in our poetry, is easily eclipsed by the naked sight of the world's beauty our absence affords. We are as motes in God's eye. With Racine as her authority, Weil declares an end to literature. She will continue to write, but writing cannot claim her heart and soul. Writing as a human being for other human beings ("To make human readers catch a glimpse . . .") is evidence of misery. Far better to prepare for the moment of illumination, when we disappear at last.

Weil, once proud to acknowledge her kinship to the seventeenth-century writers, who would have her ear be perfectly receptive to the imminent sound signaled by the movement of the violinist's bow, who is herself capable of the most memorable expression—this writer and thinker who so deeply loves art is prepared to imagine, and to welcome, a world from which the human presence, represented by the self and the imperfect forms of beauty it creates, represented by her own expendable writing, is banished—a world in which human beauty is not part of the world's beauty. There is no place for her in her own philosophy.

When she wrote these words to Bousquet, who mistook which of the texts she had sent to him was the more precious to its author, Weil was ready to undertake her research. The proposal for the front-line nurses was the script for her exit, one whose place and timing she wanted to control. Its lack of realism in terms of the conditions of combat in the Second World War does not negate its other realism as a refraction of the Europe she knew and could never bring herself spiritually to leave. The horror of that Europe she was prepared to recognize. Weil looked upon Nazi Germany as "a mirror. What we glimpse there that is so hideous is our own features, only magnified" (*EL* 102). Destroying the mirror will not cure the disease eating away at our hearts and faces; a spiritual blight of this magnitude cannot be undone by brave ministrations on the battlefield. Weil's France had fallen, and something within her had broken, completely. Weil knew as much; tired of the politics among the Free French, she sent her letter of resignation to her colleague Louis Closon: "I am finished, broken, beyond all possibility of repair, and this independently of Koch's bacilli. They have only taken advantage of the absence of resistance and, naturally, are busy demolishing a bit more" (*VSW* 685). Even the picture of escape, and of transcendence, so gallantly contrived by the imagination could not hold. Perhaps the proposal in all its verbal restraint can be approached quite simply as a moment of research into the process of obliteration, a moving lament to freedom lost and never regained.

CONCLUSION

The correct expression of a thought always produces a change within the soul; the thought is either strengthened or surpassed. For thoughts, the right expression is an ordeal. That is why the correct expression of thoughts grown to the point of maturity, even including errors, is always a good thing (before this point, always bad).

Two ordeals for thoughts: expression and doubt, that is to say, the complete silence of the whole soul for a short period of time. The second is superior by far. (*OC* 6:2:429)

Reading that astonishing document of a spiritual journey that are Weil's notebooks, one is struck again and again, not only by the range of her thoughts, but by the authority conveyed in the expression of them. These are not mere musings, although the occasional moment of sheer speculation is quickly identified as such; they are experiences lived through, pondered, measured. The life of the mind recorded at its extremest pitch, displaying its almost frightening abundance with an intensity and integrity that are searing, Weil's notebooks are the direct descendants of Pascal's *Pensées* and are also something new. For Weil, writing them became a personal obligation; one entry begins: "Make myself write in this notebook every day, even if I have failed in my duty, as has been the case today" (*OC* 6:2:427). The pressure of events and the course of a singular destiny giving rise to their creation explain, at least in part, their urgency and forceful impact; but beyond the historical, accidental circumstances of a life are forces in which the mind participates and the workings of which may be confronted in the act of

137

writing. This is the essential drama played out in Weil's writing as such; if the pages themselves are subject to flame or other cause of loss, if the books remain unread on the shelf, the intersection of the mind and the intangible truths working their way into the consciousness is precisely the point where the pen meets paper. It is a drama of absolutes. This activity of inscription, a thing of no moment to the truth itself, secure in its existence beyond the sky, has value only for us, but neither because it enables us to possess certain thoughts (they instead pass through us), nor because it allows us to act upon the world (it is we who are acted upon by the expression of these thoughts), nor even because it gives voice or a certain permanence to the self (that which is personal, the I, is only an obstacle worthy of decreation). Weil anticipates Celan's affirmation of the validity of poetic "exercises—in the *spiritual* sense" (26), to which he adds: "Poems are also gifts—gifts to the attentive" (26). Thoughts and sometimes poems ripen of themselves and fall into their given form of expression or undergo the purifying ordeal of doubt. This brief illumination, perfect or imperfect in its reflection of truth, will confirm us in our thoughts or show us their inadequacies.

In so many ways a condemnation of this unjust world (although first and foremost a call to see it clearly), Weil's Platonism enables the work of the intellect, including its indispensable manifestation in the form of writing, and makes of it an instrument of light. Is there a more optimistic note sounded anywhere in her work than where she is describing, in loving detail, the exercise of the critical faculty in the effort she has undertaken?:

> The intellect can never penetrate mystery, but it can—and it alone can—determine the suitability of the words that express it. For this use, it must be sharper, more piercing, more precise, more rigorous, and more exacting than for any other. (*OC* 6:2:460)

When citing approvingly the example of Mallarmé, Weil may well have been taking courage from his wish to "give a purer meaning to the words of the tribe" (1:38), a poetic endeavor transposed in her case to the purification of language associated with mystical experience. Her insistence on intellectual rigor and acuity corresponds to the startlingly direct and unexpected formulation of insights that so often appears in her writing. Kazin describes the effect of this disarming immediacy of tone and insight when he salutes "a charity absolutely unknown in my immediate world, an intelligence that owed nothing to authority and worldly prudence, a personal sense of God's reality and truth so natural to her that it could shock you into taking it seriously as well" (98). Bringing her intellectual and linguistic powers to bear on the study of the world as "a text with several meanings" (*OC* 6:1:295), Weil stuns the reader by the piercing light shed on the quotidian ("A man of letters humbles himself before his genius, a coquette before her beauty, a woman standing in line before an egg" [*OC* 6:2:382]), or by the intuition of the imperceptible (the unvoiced predicament of the tramp before the judge in "La Personne et le sacré" [*EL* 32]). Nothing is taken for granted; the Marseilles notebooks in particular are the text of an outsider refusing to trade the data of personal experience for received ideas or expressions. She examines the evidence afresh.

Writing is a *via negativa*: "Writing—like translating—negative— pushing away those words that obscure the model, the silent thing that must be expressed" (*OC* 6:1:302). Writing, so defined, must be all of a piece, corresponding to its single inspiration; at the same time, it is accomplished by means of a principle of exclusion, countering the mind's suggestibility to language. Writing that honors its subject in this way is known by the characteristics of integrity, refusal of obscurity, and a certain astringency, all cultivated by Weil with the zeal of the seeker of the truth. Any kind of facility is suspect; expansiveness is suspect: "Like gas, the soul tends to occupy the full volume of the space it is given" (*OC* 6:2:285). But it is not the self that writing serves to express. The unvoiced referent, *la chose muette*, is silent; it wants, not impression or ornament, but its perfect equivalent in words. Weil's linguistic idealism, so far removed in tenor from theory today, may be anachronistic, but it is so in the same way as is, for example, her lament for the Cathars; it may be understood as posing in its time an alternative space immune to otherwise all-pervasive pressures to conform to a corrupt and disgraceful ideology: "Languedoc. Nothing is worth a dead, unrevivable country (no great beast)" (*C* 3:64). Scourged by doubt and the systematic rejection of all unnecessary words, thoughts secure their tangible existence at last.

Philosophical reflection uses language as a means, not an end:

The subject of philosophy is *real*. It isn't just words, it isn't a fiction. But this subject is real only in relation to thought ... Neither is it an art as Valéry said, because the artist creates things that have value, and the philosopher reflects on value. However, in order to communicate his thought, he has to make a work of art out of words (indirect expression). (*OC* 6:1:174)

Being of a higher degree of abstraction than art, philosophy creates its intellectual drama not out of words and all they might evoke, but rather out of thoughts inspired by the study of values, necessarily taking shape in words. Words are not the substance of this drama; they are its effect and manifestation. If they rank lower than thought on the implicit scale, this does not redound to the glory of the philosophers who wield them; the secondary rank of language means not that philosophers are superior, but that the written expression of thoughts is ultimately expendable. Ideas exist independently of our efforts. A work of literature that is destroyed—that has no copies, that no one has memorized—is permanently lost. Literature depends on language for its existence; philosophy depends on language only for its expression. In a sense, all our words are superfluous. In a universe where God exists, we ourselves are superfluous—a thought expressed in one of Weil's most comic, and bitter, asides: "'Folly of love.' The creation is a much bigger folly than the incarnation" (*OC* 6:2:368). The nature of her written *œuvre* and the thought haunting it and no doubt impelling it into existence are at heart one and the same.

And yet Weil did believe in the practical value of philosophical work and expression, at least for the philosopher: "Philosophy— search for wisdom—is a virtue. It is an effort on the self. A transformation of being" (*OC* 6:1:174). We cannot change the world beyond the sky, but, by aligning ourselves with it, we can change ourselves. And there exists a good reason for creating a record of the effort, one that overrules the essential difference between literature and philosophy with respect to language:

The highest stimulus is: if I don't do it, it will not exist. Work of art; it's an obvious example. The work I do not create, no one else will ever create it. But I don't have the choice between several works of art. Similarly for any great thing. And if a certain person does not write a certain poem, I will never read it. The same for a good deed.

I am only an intermediary, but an indispensable one. (*OC* 6:2:298)

Again, an affirmation associated with, among other things, the act of writing. Perhaps it should not so astonish us that one able to radically question the necessity of existence should leave behind so much; silence, in this case, would be acquiescence. Weil wanted justice to, as she saw it, descend.

What of the personal work—that "effort on the self"—she hoped to accomplish through her reflection and writing? Perhaps the notebooks can be read as the record of a decreation: "We possess nothing on earth—for chance can take everything away—except for the power to say 'I.' That is what we must offer to God—that is to say, destroy. There is absolutely no other free act that is granted us, only the destruction of the 'I'" (*OC* 6:2:461). In a way, Weil is writing a book from which she would be absent, in imitation of her God, just as Balzac, writing *La Comédie Humaine* a century earlier, entered into friendly rivalry with his. But there is nothing gently ironic about Weil's enterprise. She is not a fictional character in search of the absolute; everything is at stake. The many passages delving into utter deprivation, the focus on the crucifixion, the recurrent analysis of might and its effects, the insistence of the finite nature of evil, and the similar themes sounded repeatedly thoughout the notebooks written in France all point to the desperate search within for thoughts equal to the reality she was living through, all she sensed so acutely in the times. That her thought took on a Christian and mystical cast anathema to some and perhaps too blithely appropriated by others does not erase the fact that this is no triumphant record, but a heartrending one, in the shaping of which the tragic injustices of her time and culture played their part. Often she thinks of the final scene of *Phèdre*:

And death, withdrawing clarity from my sight,
Gives back all its purity to once-sullied light. (1:876)

Human existence is a blot on the universe. There is no other way to construe the evidence. Perhaps one can turn elsewhere: "Who knows whether the conversion and silence of Racine are not due to these two verses?" (C 3:37). Does Weil's *œuvre*, an offshoot of that same language of Racine and Pascal, implicate another conversion and silence, fraught with difficulties, in the occupied France of three centuries later? What claim on the imagination of readers can her ringing words have in a postwar world where the book is being unceremoniously dethroned?

Like all works of literature that let the mind live more fully, more intensely, her work, startling and eloquent, would leave us poorer by its absence. But its riches are like the shards of a precious vessel, not polished jewels. A journey that begins by questioning the fitness of the world for human habitation ends by questioning the fitness of human habitation in the world anywhere. The thirst for justice is absorbed by silence. Perspective is withdrawn:

> The beauty of a landscape at the moment when no one sees it, absolutely no one . . .
> To see a landscape such as it is when I am not there.
> When I am somewhere, I sully the silence of heaven and earth with my breathing and the beating of my heart. (C 3:38)

The struggle with breath and heartbeat—our human noise—is the stuff of life, and it was the price of Weil's spiritual adventure. Poetry, as Tsvetaeva reminds us, inhabits only "[t]he low close sky of the earth" (166). The poetic thinking so apparent in Weil's written work tells us that, on this bottom rung of the ladder she has positioned toward a Platonic and mystical truth, she cannot climb above the requirements of style and perspective, above the contradictions and impingements of a life lived amid the landscapes of history. For this reason, her disquieting work has the power to move us beyond its pages, replete with beautiful illuminations and touched by shadows, and into the nearby silences where her words resonate still.

WORKS CITED

WORKS BY SIMONE WEIL

Attente de Dieu. Paris: Fayard, 1966.
Cahiers. New ed. 3 vols. Paris: Plon, 1970–74.
La Condition ouvrière. Paris: Gallimard, 1951.
La Connaissance surnaturelle. Paris: Gallimard, 1950.
Correspondance [with Joë Bousquet]. Lausanne: l'Age d'Homme, 1982.
"Deux lettres inédites à Joë Bousquet." *Cahiers Simone Weil* 19:2 (1996): 137–53.
Ecrits de Londres et dernières lettres. Paris: Gallimard, 1957.
L'Enracinement. Paris: Gallimard, 1949.
"Lettre aux *Cahiers du Sud* sur les responsabilités de la littérature." *Cahiers Simone Weil* 10:4 (1987): 354–57.
"Morale et littérature." *Cahiers Simone Weil* 10:4 (1987): 349–53.
Œuvres complètes. Ed. André A. Devaux and Florence de Lussy. 6 vols. to date. Paris: Gallimard, since 1988.
Poèmes, suivis de Venise sauvée. Paris: Gallimard, 1968.

OTHER WORKS

Baudelaire, Charles. *Œuvres complètes.* 2 vols. Paris: Gallimard, 1975–76.

Benjamin, Walter. *Illuminations.* Ed. Hannah Arendt. New York: Schocken, 1969.

Bishop, Elizabeth. *The Complete Poems, 1927–1979.* New York: Farrar, Straus and Giroux, 1983.

Brodsky, Joseph. *On Grief and Reason.* New York: Farrar, Straus and Giroux, 1995.

Celan, Paul. *Collected Prose.* Trans. Rosmarie Waldrop. Manchester: Carcanet, 1986.

Char, René. *Œuvres complètes.* Paris: Gallimard, 1983.

Coles, Robert. *Simone Weil: A Modern Pilgrimage.* Reading, MA: Addison-Wesley, 1987.

Courtivron, Isabelle de. "Rebel Without a Cause." *The New York Times Book Review* (December 14, 1997): 14–15

Devaux, André A. "Simone Weil et Blaise Pascal." *Sud* 87/88 (1990): 75–99.

———. "Simone Weil professeur au-delà de sa classe." *Cahiers Simone Weil* 20:1 (1997): 27–47.

Dickinson, Emily. *The Letters of Emily Dickinson.* 3 vols. Cambridge, MA: Belknap, 1986.

Evans, Christine Ann. "The Nature of Narrative in Simone Weil's Vision of History: The Need for New Historical Roots" in John M. Dunaway and Eric O. Springsted, eds. *The Beauty That Saves: Essays on Aesthetics and Language in Simone Weil.* Macon: Mercer UP, 1996.

———. "The Power of Parabolic Reversal: The Example in Simone Weil's Notebooks." *Cahiers Simone Weil* 19:3 (1996): 313–24.

Fiori, Gabriella. *Simone Weil: une femme absolue.* Paris: du Félin, 1987.

Glück, Louise. *Proofs and Theories.* Hopewell, NJ: Ecco, 1995.

Havel, Václav. *Living in Truth.* Ed. Jan Vladislav. London: Faber and Faber, 1987.

Heaney, Seamus. *The Redress of Poetry.* New York: Farrar, Straus and Giroux, 1995.

Irigaray, Luce. *Speculum de l'autre femme.* Paris: Minuit, 1974.

Isaac, Jeffrey C. *Arendt, Camus, and Modern Rebellion.* New Haven: Yale UP, 1992.

Jacob, Max. *Conseils à un jeune poète.* Paris: Gallimard, 1972.

John of the Cross. *The Collected Works of St. John of the Cross.* Trans. Kieran Kavanaugh, O.C.D. and Otilio Rodriquez, O.C.D. Washington, DC: ICS, 1979.

Kahn, Gilbert. "Le Style narratif." *Cahiers Simone Weil* 10:4 (1987): 379–82.

Kaplan, Alice Yaeger. *Reproductions of Banality: Fascism, Literature, and French Intellectual Life.* Minneapolis: U of Minnesota, 1986.

Kazin, Alfred. *Writing Was Everything*. Cambridge: Harvard UP, 1995.

La Fontaine, Jean de. *Œuvres complètes*. 1 vol. to date. Paris: Gallimard, 1991.

Le Dœuff, Michèle. *Hipparchia's Choice: An Essay Concerning Women, Philosophy, Etc.* Trans. Trista Selous. Oxford: Blackwell, 1991.

Little, J. P. "Simone Weil, ou la pensée analogique." *Sud* 87/88 (1990): 51–60.

Lussy, Florence de. "Paul Valéry et Simone Weil." *Cahiers Simone Weil* 17:4 (1994): 407–29.

McCarthy, Patrick. "Clown, Prophet, Saint." *Times Literary Supplement* (July 13–19, 1990): 770.

McLellan, David. *Utopian Pessimist: The Life and Thought of Simone Weil*. New York: Simon & Schuster, 1990.

Mallarmé, Stéphane. *Œuvres complètes*. New ed. 1 vol. to date. Paris: Gallimard, 1998.

Milosz, Czeslaw. *The Witness of Poetry*. Cambridge: Harvard UP, 1983.

Moi, Toril. *Simone de Beauvoir: The Making of an Intellectual Woman*. Cambridge, MA: Blackwell, 1994.

Nevin, Thomas R. *Simone Weil: Portrait of a Self-Exiled Jew*. Chapel Hill: U of North Carolina Press, 1991.

O'Connor, Flannery. *The Habit of Being*. New York: Farrar, Straus and Giroux, 1979.

Oxenhandler, Neal. *Looking for Heroes in Postwar France*. Hanover: UP of New England, 1996.

Pascal, Blaise. *Œuvres complètes*. Paris: Gallimard, 1954.

Pétrement, Simone. *La Vie de Simone Weil*. New ed. Paris: Fayard, 1997.

Racine, Jean. *Œuvres complètes*. New ed. 1 vol to date. Paris: Gallimard, 1999.

Reynolds, Siân. *France Between the Wars: Gender and Politics*. London: Routledge, 1996.

Rimbaud, Arthur. *Œuvres complètes*. Paris: Gallimard, 1972.

Springsted, Eric O. *Simone Weil and the Suffering of Love*. Cambridge, MA: Cowley, 1986.

Steiner, George. *No Passion Spent*. New Haven: Yale UP, 1996.

Stevens, Wallace. *Collected Poetry and Prose*. New York: Library of America, 1997.

Tsvetaeva, Marina. *Art in the Light of Conscience*. Trans. Angela Livingstone. Cambridge: Harvard UP, 1992.

Vetö, Miklos. *The Religious Metaphysics of Simone Weil*. Trans. Joan Dargan. Albany: SUNY Press, 1994.

Weil, André. "Propos sur Simone Weil (entretien avec Malcolm Muggeridge)." *Sud* 87/88 (1990): 9–23.

———. *Souvenirs d'apprentissage*. Basel: Birkhäuser, 1991.

Weitz, Margaret Collins. *Sisters in the Resistance: How Women Fought to Free France, 1940–1945*. New York: John Wiley and Sons, 1995.

INDEX